WHY WE GO HUNTING

The unexpected pleasures of a
hunting trip are what we remember
most of nature and wildlife

By Solbert

To order additional copies of this book, contact:
Xlibris Corporation
1-888-795-4274
www.Xlibris.com
Orders@Xlibris.com
28069

Preface

The original reason for "Hunting" was plainly for survival. Today, there are still people in the world that hunt for survival. It is a necessity in their case they have to have food. People in our civilized world "go hunting" for a variety of reasons.

Here are a few main reasons:

- It is a way to keep the population of wild animals under control.
- It provides enormous amounts of money used for the many parks, and national and regional offices maintained by the bureau of wildlife management which in turn control and manage the local divisions of wildlife, issues the licenses and decides how many of a certain species of wildlife can and should be killed off each year to maintain a good healthy herd.
- Every State that sells "Hunting" licenses contributes to the above.
- Maintaining a healthy number of each and every species of wildlife is important and it must be done to keep the species alive.

Not every species of wildlife are hunted. Licenses are issued for hunting and trapping only in the cases where the population is not endangered or there is overpopulation.

The cost of licenses pertaining to wildlife range from very few dollars to several thousands of dollars for hunting permits around the world

Personal reasons are:

- We like the outdoors.
- We enjoy the many beautiful sights we encounter on a "hunt".
- We like to see the wildlife and watch them in their own habitat. Not just what we are pursuing, but what we can see as we pursue our prey.
- We like the unexpected things that can and do happen on our "hunt".
- We like the challenge of trying to outwit the prey we are after, sometimes we win, but many more times we lose, we still enjoy the "hunt".

Without Game management, some species would soon become over the population number that the habitat could support, starvation would begin and the herd would suffer much starvation and death.

To the reader:

I received my first single shot 22-caliber rifle at the age of nine years, nineteen twenty-nine. I have had a variety of guns ever since, a period of seventy-five years. I've had no accidents. I have spent a lot of time in the woods, fields etc. that I will tell you about in the chapters of this book. This world is covered with a lot of beauty, Unbelievable in it's vastness, and design. I wish I could see more.

There is a never-ending cycle of life and death in everything on this earth, from the two hundred foot trees in the Jungle to the smallest of insects. I will tell you of some of the many pleasant, and sometimes terrifying things I have seen during those seventy-five years.

All of the opinions and statements made or alluded to in this book are my own and may not be entirely true to actual fact, but close as I remember them.

The animals I encountered in foreign countries were new to me and I did not know the names of some of them. The trees were also not familiar to me.

I just want to tell you that "hunting" is not about just chasing an animal and killing it. Trying to outwit a canny old white tailed deer and get close enough for a clean shot is very challenging and does not happen that often. It is the chase and the beauty of the area that is rewarding, not the kill.

Why Do We Hunt?

Good question? From only a relatively short time ago, back through hundreds of years, even thousands of years ago people on this earth hunted out of pure necessity. Even today somewhere in this world, someone is still hunting to exist.

Hunting in order to live is still done, even in this United States, though few and far between. Most hunting in the USA is now licensed and controlled, and is now done mostly for the pleasure of the hunter. A large percentage of the hunters, hunt and keep the particular game for the freezer and meat through the winter.

The thousands of dollars collected from the license fees are used by the Government to alleviate the cost of everything from Parks to managing the game population and paying the forest rangers, among other things.

In my humble opinion, the main reason we like to hunt is for the many pleasures we get when we enter the natural world, the smell of the pine trees, the little animals that move about. If a hunter is quiet, he sees much.

To "hunt" is for the sheer pleasure of just being out there in the natural things that we see as we roam the hills, fields, desert, or whatever. Of course a lot of the time we are going after a particular animal or thing, whatever it may be, to take home and put in the freezer. Some hunters are trophy hunters and are looking for an animal that is the best of the species. They will take it home, put the meat in the freezer and the Antlers on the wall to look at occasionally and remember the pleasant experience of the whole trip, not just the killing of the animal.

To hunt for a special animal on the western plains and finally take it is a very strong challenge. Locating them is hard to do in the first place. Then tracking them is time consuming and takes a lot of stamina and courage. Remember you are in their home territory and they are familiar with every hill and valley. You must not be seen or heard or they will be long gone when you get to where you think they are.

A hunter comes back empty handed a lot more times than he gets his quarry.

If you ask a returning hunter if he enjoyed the hunt he will undoubtedly say yes, not getting what he went after does not mean he did not enjoy the hunt.

Animal Alertness

He may not mention the beautiful birds he saw gathering seeds to eat or the squirrels that he saw running through the tree tops to get back to their nest to hide. He also may not mention the red Fox that crossed his path when he was silently going down a hillside. Maybe he would not mention the large red tailed Hawk that circled overhead watching to see what he would scare up that it could catch. He would not mention the time that he put his foot down and almost stepped on a rattlesnake.

All those things he will remember and think back to that time. If it was in the fall of the year, he will remember the sound of leaves falling, the color changes in the many different kinds of wild flowers, the green color leaving the grass, leaves flower stems etc. These things are all things of beauty to the observer and make the "hunt" so pleasant a memory.

Along with all that are also the stillness and the ever-present fact that at any moment something could appear or happen. When a Grouse is resting in the woods, it is usually on the ground. The coloring of its feathers are so good and match the grass or leaves so well that it is very hard to see. Sometimes the grouse will set there on the ground until you are within two or three feet of it before it will take off. When it does it comes up with a roar of its wings that will startle the bravest of hunters. When a hunter walks into the woods, he automatically slows down and starts walking silently, making as little noise as possible. He listens for any sound that may signal some kind of activity ahead. He watches ahead as far as he can and notices the activity of the birds, squirrels etc, to see what they are doing. The birds and animals know each other's ways and sounds and when one of them does something out of the ordinary they all notice and act accordingly.

When I am sitting in a stand and waiting for a deer I am listening and watching the birds and squirrels around me. I can tell from their actions when another hunter or strange animal is coming this way. They know I am there, but if I am not moving they ignore me. The common Blue Jay is a real alarm system. The minute one of them sees a strange animal or human, they let out a loud scream that can be heard several hundred yards away. I have been watching deer when another hunter or animal came into the area and a Blue Jay screamed a warning. The Deer's head and ears came up instantly and it acted accordingly. Blue Jays will sometimes give a false alarm, but the other birds and animals will still become alert and check around. It may be a dog, fox, bear, coyote, man, or even a cat or Hawk. Anything different will be noticed and the alarm will be given. If it appears non-aggressive they will go back to whatever they were doing. If you are sitting in your stand and watching the birds and squirrels and suddenly they are gone, you can bet something is coming into the area. Just sit still and soon you will see one of the predator groups. Be it man or animal, they went into hiding till they were sure of just what it was. Their lives depend on their seeing the predator before it sees them. The next time you see a group of Canadian geese, anywhere. Just look at the group, there will always be at least one, just standing guard and watching.

Wild or even domestic animals are very intelligent and can sense, feel and in a lot of cases see a change in attitude in a person or another animal. The next time you go outside to feed your pet, smile as you go toward it. When you are half way to the food dish, just change your expression and frown or look angry towards it. The animal will quickly stop and get poised to flee or hide from you. It picked up the angry signal as soon as you showed it on your face and in your eyes.

The crows I used to hunt got very wise. If I started from the house with the long stick (my gun) in my arms, they would soon start talking back and forth and I could not get within range of them. I had to learn to keep the gun along side of my leg till I entered the forest when they were where they could see me as I left the house.

Many times the different animals pass each other in the woods and just keep to their own paths as they go on their ways, unless of course they are hunter and prey. In which case the prey had better see the hunter first and take to cover quickly. Each animal, bird and even insects are always looking for movement around them. If it is something that they know and are not afraid of, they continue on their way. If it is an enemy, they hide or run, being alert all the time is life or death to them.

Memorable Incidents

At the extreme left of my area of vision I noticed a slight movement. I never moved a hair. Slowly a large raccoon came into view. Behind it, in a neat line came three little raccoons. They were spaced about six inches apart and following their mother's path.

There was a fallen log about six feet in front of where I had chosen to sit and put my back against a large stump. I was dressed in fall camouflage coveralls and a camo hat with a facemask made of see-thru material.

The mother raccoon climbed up on the log at the end, the young ones followed suit and they all paraded down the log in front of me and off the other end and proceeded on toward wherever they were going.

They never even glanced toward me as they went by. Those young ones were beautiful little things. I know people that have received permission from the game wardens to keep them as pets. They later released them because they never really get tame. They are still wild animals and can turn against you if you do something they don't like. If you try to take their food, for whatever reason, they will react as they would in the wild—it is their instinct. You could easily be bitten or worse. Even pet dogs, have turned on their master and attacked. Every year children and adults are bitten by pets. We must remember they once were wild and still have the instinct to fight.

In the northeastern states, the raccoons have, for the last few years at least, been infected with Rabies. The wildlife people have responded well, using aircraft, they have dropped treated marshmallows in the infected areas to fight the Rabies infection. I have not heard how it has worked, but the number of infected raccoons seems to have dropped. It appears that when they are infected, they lose their fear of man or anything else and become very aggressive. That is why all children that live in areas where there are many raccoons must be told not to approach any wild animal that is not afraid of them or is acting strangely.

Occasionally I have seen foxes with rabies. They did not run from my car as I approached them on the highway. Just stood and looked at my car as it approached. I had to drive off of the highway a little to get around them, and they growled as I went by. On two of them, there was a white foamy froth around their mouths, so I knew they had rabies and called the Game Warden.

A large Fox squirrel sat on the end of the log for a while looking around, then proceeded to take twelve inch hops up the log toward where I was sitting along side of it with my back against the tree stump.

Every other hop or two he would stop, sit up, and flip his beautiful tail a time or two, and then start hopping again.

Finally he stopped on the log at the spot where my large boot was leaning against the log. He flipped his tail again while he was looking at me. He was not sure what he was looking at. Then he hopped over on the toe of my boot, flipping his tail all the time now. He evidently did not like the feel of the object he was sitting on, for he suddenly jumped back to the log and ran back down to the end, where he flipped his tail again and barked a warning to the rest of the forest that something was not exactly right. He jumped off the log and ran up passed me and on about his business.

A Fox squirrel is a beautiful little animal and his tail is as large as the rest of his body beautifully colored. Most are over a foot in length. He uses his tail as an umbrella if he gets caught in the rain and wants to keep on eating and it is not raining too hard. There are several different sizes of squirrels and they seem to stay with the species. There are fox squirrels, gray squirrels, black squirrels, red squirrels, ground squirrels etc, and they do not seem to intermix. The black squirrels, I hear, have moved down from our neighbors to the north, from Canada. They are a very beautiful little animal and are completely black in color, and about the same size as our gray squirrel.

Internationally speaking there are probably hundreds of different squirrels, of all shapes and sizes and colors. Any nature lover that will take the time to go into a wooded or even a dessert area and just sit still for a few minutes or so, will probably see some kind of squirrel start moving around somewhere. The little ground squirrels are nearly everywhere, even into some of the suburban areas and villages.

I do not know of any squirrel that is a meat eater. There may be some in other countries, but I have not heard of them. Most are vegetarians and nut eaters. Of course, this takes in the eating of the fresh buds in the spring and the seedeaters of the fall month. They are all hunted by the predator groups, the Owls, Hawks, snakes, lizards and anything that is a predator of small animals like Coyotes, cats etc. I imagine that a very large percentage of the young of the squirrel species is food for the predator groups. The large percentage taken for food does not seem to effect the living population in any way.

Whitetail Deer

I saw the young buck as I rounded the curve in the trail, on my way down off the high hill I had went up earlier in the day. It was standing about ten feet off of the trail I was coming down. When I first saw it I used my field glasses to see what it was. I saw that it was a young buck with only about two inches of antler growth and it was not on my list of eligible deer.

A few more steps and it either heard me or caught a whiff of my scent. It turned it's head and looked at me as I walked down the trail toward it. I kept my eyes on the trail and just kept on walking, with my peripheral vision I could see how beautiful the young buck was. Not making eye contact with the eyes of the young buck It never moved until I was passing it, then it just turned it's head to watch me go on down the trail.

When I was about a hundred feet or so passed it and still going, I turned my head and looked back. This time I looked into it's eyes. It just stood there and watched as I went on down the trail. I kept glancing back to see if it would run, but it did not. It just started walking a little slowly further away from the trail.

It walked off into the woods still unafraid. If I had made eye contact when I was walking past it, it would have probably snorted and ran off as fast as it could. It thought I had not seen it and it did not move so that I would see it.

That little fact, not making eye contact has taken me very close to many animals. Rabbits especially will sometimes sit in a clump of grass and let you step within a foot of them, as long as you do not make eye contact, and keep a steady pace. Even the larger animals, if they see you and they believe you do not see them, will just stand there and watch you go by. If you look at them and make eye contact, they have to respond, one way or another. Of course there are times when they will jump and run just because you are coming toward them and they are afraid. Many will leave when they first hear you. I imagine it depends on their past experiences with humans. It sometimes depends on the angle you are approaching. If you are walking directly toward them, they will run immediately. If you are approaching from an angle and it looks like you will pass them a little distance away, they may just stay still and let you go by. The deer on the color plate is a mature ten-point buck in its prime, what the average hunter is hoping to see and harvest. They generally control a large area of wherever they are born and have been living. They do most of the breeding and therefore keep a good healthy herd of deer in the area.

The stalking and shooting of a Deer this size is rare in most areas. I have not seen the statistics, but at the local check-in station only one or two Deer of this size is weighed in each year. Some years, none are brought in. There may be lots of two, four or six pointers brought in, even some eight pointers, but the big boys keep ahead of the hunters. Some of the tricks they pull to avoid the hunters will amaze you. They have been known to hide under the overhang of a riverbank, in the water with only their head above water, until they thought it was safe to come out. That is if the water was deep enough. They have been found next to a farmer's barn, hiding in the deep grass, and they will stay there all through the daylight hours, until they can leave in the dark. They seem to know that the hunters will not come and hunt them there. They only become a "Trophy" by being smarter than the hunters that hunt them. Most of the trophy size white tail deer that are killed are killed during the "rut". The "rut" is a short period of time in the fall of the year when the female deer become receptive to mating with the bucks. They stake out a territory (so to speak). They scrape a spot on the ground with their front hooves. Then they urinate on the spot to identify themselves. They scrape several spots in their "territory" and use their antlers to mark several small trees in the same area. Scent glands on their antlers and head leave their personal scent on the scraped trees for the females to identify them. When the female comes to a scrape and identifies the buck she wants, she in turn urinates on the scrape. Thus she tells the buck she is in the area and is available. When the buck checks the scrape for visiting females and finds a new female has been to one of his scrapes, he immediately follows her hoof scent trail to find her.

He will fight any other buck that enters the area and tries to mate with any of his current herd of females that are in the area. He will chase any interfering buck out of the area, and being the largest buck with the biggest antlers in the area. Most of the younger bucks will leave him alone. Thus the herd of deer in that area will always be good and healthy and will produce more strong healthy bucks.

The damage to the young trees is sometimes pretty costly to the tree farmer and could be in hundreds of dollars.

Early Hunting Years

Before I had received the little single shot .22-caliber rifle, I used a homemade sling. The sling was made up of an eighteen inch piece of rubber cut from an old car inner-tube about 1/2 inch wide, a two inch round piece of leather cut from the tongue of an old shoe and a twelve inch piece of strong cord. I cut two little holes opposite each other in the round piece of leather, tied the two ends of the cord to the holes, put a slip noose at the middle of the cord, slipped it over the end of the strip of rubber and I had me a good sling.

I became very good with the sling, even hitting running rabbits within a seventy foot range. I received a good spanking, when I was seven or eight because I killed a robin by accident. It was in the cherry tree eating ripe cherries and I just brought up the sling instinctively and shot a stone to scare the bird away. The stone hit the bird in the head and my father just happened to be watching.

I loved to roam the woods with the sling. After school, I would do my evening chores, then head to the creek or the woods with my sling. Many a turtle or snake felt the sting of a small stone, and many snakes were killed. I hated snakes and spiders and I killed as many as I could whenever I could. One late summer day there was nothing that I was needed for so I ask my mother if I could go for a hike in the woods. I always had my sling in my pocket so with her permission I started off.

I walked fast until I entered the trees. Then I slowed down and started my quiet walk. I had been shown how to walk in the woods without making much noise. My older brother was a good teacher and he taught me much about the woods and hunting, and I became quite good, except when the leaves were falling in the fall and they were dry. Nothing could go through them without making a little noise, mostly just a slight rustling. There were no dry leaves, at least not new ones and the ones that were there had been pressed into the ground and would not make any noise if stepped on right.

I moved slowly up the little hill that was near the edge of the wooded area, watching ahead for any movement that would indicate some animal or bird.

As I neared the top where I could start to see anything that might be on the other side of the hill, my pulse quickened and as usual I became expectant. I thought to myself, what is going to be there? It could be anything. In my young mind, I imagined everything up to a bear. At that time there were no deer in the state of Ohio, and I had never seen one, so I never gave them any thought. There were no Bears either, but my young mind was ready for anything. I crept quietly on up to the crest of the hill.

As I neared the top of the hill I passed a large tree stump that was rotting away. It was just high enough that when I sat down the top of my head would be just below the top of the stump and my head would not be silhouetted against the skyline behind me. So I sat down with my sling in my lap and waited to see what would show up.

I had already learned how to sit still for long periods of time without moving. Except for an occasional itch, which would not go away, I seldom moved. If I sat for any length of time and nothing appeared, then I would slowly move my arm and hand to scratch or maybe move my leg from a cramped position, then I would be still again.

After about ten or fifteen minutes of unmoving time had gone by, I was startled as a huge bird came flying in and landed about twenty feet from where I was sitting. My heart was pounding and I just sat there and looked at it.

The bird that had landed, I had seen one before when my older brother had gone pheasant hunting and brought one home. The bird was a male pheasant with beautiful feathers all over his body and the long tail feathers were pointed up and were blowing in the soft breeze. The sun was still up high enough that it was shinning on him as he stood there looking at me.

I hadn't moved a muscle, but he looked at me I was sure. He stood there still as a rock as I looked at him I thought, "Boy, is he ever beautiful" with bright reds, blues, and the bright white markings, especially the white ring around his neck. All shaded the way they were in the sunlight, was something to see. The long tail feathers in their shades of brown tan and with the black markings were something to behold. I had never seen a live one that close before and I was truly amazed. As he stood there trying to figure out just what I was, my heart was beating a mile a minute and I did not feel any cramps or itches whatever.

He finally decided that I was something he did not want to be near and he ran down the back side of the hill and on into some tall grasses that were in the bottom of the ravine that was there

I moved then, and found out that my muscles were a little cramped, but I had not noticed it before, and I was shaking a little from the close encounter with such a beautiful wild thing. I had forgotten my sling in the excitement of the moment. I would not have shot at such a beautiful bird anyway, I thought. That was a moment to remember. When I told my mother about it, she just smiled and said "I'm glad'".

Even a color picture will not do the pheasant justice; it is so beautiful in full color that you must see it to believe it. I hope that if you have never seen one, you will somehow get a chance. As for me, I believe the ring-necked pheasant to be one of the most beautiful of birds. The ring neck pheasant shown in the color plate in the front of this book is being held by my grandson. It was struck by a car and he took it in for a few days and fed and took care of it till it was ready to go on it's own. They become very tame quickly when they find out that you will not bother them. Several people in this area buy eggs, hatch them and raise the young, and then when they are old enough they release them into the wild. This process helps the population considerably and I think it is necessary for the future of the bird. My grandson enjoyed taking care of the beautiful bird for about a week.

He released it back into the woods and fields behind his house as soon as it could walk and fly ok. You can see by the coloring and looks of it that it is a very beautiful bird. There are not many of them around here, due I think to the many predators. There are fox, coyotes, hawks, and cats that have turned wild, bobcats and skunks, that love the eggs in the spring. The pheasants really do not have much chance to make it to full growth. To add to that, they nest in the thick grasses of the farmers hay and clover fields and when the farmer harvests his crop of hay early in order to get a second harvest. He unknowingly destroys the nest of eggs that was hidden in the clover or hay.

Many things help to destroy the propagation of the ring-necked pheasant. The fox, coyote, skunk, weasel hawks and other predators, all play a part in hindering the population growth of the bird. They are not an endangered bird as yet, but it may be coming.

Several times in my hunting forays, I have seen different predators catch and kill other birds or animals and insects. It is an everyday happening in nature. The meat eaters have to eat to survive and their only food is another animal or bird. The red tailed hawk that swoops down and grabs a young rabbit with it's claws and flies off to a tree limb to eat it or the alligator that grabs a pet dog that came to the edge of the pond to drink and drags it to it's den to eat, are all doing what is natural for them. They have to eat to live and any living thing that is available is the prey that they are seeking.

Thousands of birds and small animals are killed every day to feed the predators and thousands of birds and animals are born and hatched to replace them.

Birds of Prey

The word "PREY" in the dictionary has several different meanings. There are two that fit what I am talking about. Number two is, "An animal hunted or killed for food by another animal". Number three is; "A person or thing that falls victim to someone or some thing."

A good reference is the term "Birds of Prey." Most of you over the age of five have probably heard someone say that. It simply means and refers to a group of birds that live off of other birds and small animals, they are simply faster and quicker and can catch the other birds and eat them; most of them eat the prey as soon as they are caught.

Nearly every living thing is prey to something larger or, in a few cases, smaller, that is looking for it to eat. It appears to be nature's way of keeping control over the population of any species. Most of the small animals and birds that are caught by the predators do not suffer much. When they are caught, the sharp talons of the predator penetrate the body of the prey and kill it nearly instantly.

Every day there are hundreds of birds, insects etc. that are killed and eaten by other birds insects and animals

Sometime during the summer, if you see a beautiful Bluebird, sit quiet and still for a few minutes and you will see him leave his perch and fly out in a sort of circle. Somewhere in that circle he will grab a flying insect and take it back to his nest or just to a limb of a tree and then eat the insect himself.

They are very good at keeping insects out of the garden while it is growing. Most times they sit on a post or tree limb and watch for insects on the ground.

Then he will fly to the ground and pick it up and eat it right there or maybe take it back to the nest for a young one to eat. They are very nice to have around the yard. They are very territorial and if you put up too many bluebird houses they will claim several within their range, and keep all other bluebirds out. They do eat a lot of insects though. The blue birds and other insect eating birds around human habitats are dying a lot also. It is because of the humans spraying poison around their houses to kill the mosquitoes, ants, roaches, crickets, etc. Some places they even spray the whole yard with insect killer. Those yards are eating places of robins, bluebirds, flycatchers, flickers, yellowhammers and a host of other birds. When they eat the dying insects, they also eat the poison on or in the insect, and then they die also, if the poison is strong enough. A lot of beautiful birds die that way, not intentionally, but die nevertheless.

One thing I want to mention is the number of times a hunter will see beautiful birds as they go about their daily business of staying alive. I have seen everything from the large highflying turkey vultures and red tailed hawks to the small speedster the humming bird in all his brilliant colors. They are too numerous to mention them all, but sooner or later a hunter will see them all, at least all the varieties in his area of the country.

The one I like to look for is the "pileated woodpecker." It is a very large bird, fourteen to eighteen inches (approx.) in length. Very beautiful and has a funny way of flying'. As it flies, it does not fly like other birds. It flies like one of us would row a boat. We give a large stroke; bring the oars back, and then stroke again. The pileated does that and so it goes up then coasts down, then goes up and coasts down. Its flight path is like the ocean surface when the waves are about three feet high. It has a long beak and its head is black and white with a brilliant red crown on top. The rest of the body is black with white under the wings and a few spots on the body, very beautiful.

When it finds a tree with carpenter ants, it can hear them working when they are inside a tree, it will cut a hole in to them and eat them. When it is cutting the hole you can hear the hammering for a long distance.

There are many birds to be seen if you sit quietly and just observe. You will probably see hawks. You can tell when there is a hawk approaching. All the other birds will disappear and the woods will become very quiet until it leaves the area. You will see cardinals, robins, and all sorts of sparrows, nearly all the same color, but with variations of pattern, catbirds, black wing redbirds and red winged blackbirds, Indigo buntings, a favorite of mine. It is solid blue and a very pretty shade of blue too. Mocking birds, finches, flickers crows, some species of swallow, depending on where you are. Of course you will see the noisy blue jay. You will probably hear him before you see him, if it is a sunny day. He has some days when he is quiet and you hardly know he is there. I never figured that out, unless it was due to his building a nest somewhere.

There are so many different birds; they are too numerous to mention here, the cedar waxwing, the meadowlarks, grouse, quail etc. You will see them all over a period of time if you are watchful and quiet. You will see the flycatchers, flying hither and yon as they catch the insects out of the air and consume them.

If you look up you will probably see the huge turkey vulture circling gracefully on the air currents waiting for the scent of a dead road kill or some other unfortunate animal that is dead. It is said that a vulture can smell a dead thing up to sixteen miles away and go to it for a meal. Thanks to them, when anything is killed on the highways, it does not last long unless it is a large animal. Sometimes when there are a lot of kills, it takes a lot longer than normal, but they will clean it up eventually, they are nature's garbage collectors.

Getting back to why we hunt. One season, during the bow hunting only part, I walked quietly into the area I wanted to sit and watch for a wayward deer. I found a spot under a young pine tree and when I was seated comfortably, I pulled the camo mask down over my face and glasses and waited for something to happen. It wasn't long until something came in from my left at a fairly steep angle and landed on the ground I had not seen any activity in that area so I was curious as to what was going on. I sat still and waited and looked.

I took out my field glasses slowly and looked where the thing had landed. There was a "Goshawk" standing on a small log and picking at a small ground squirrel, tearing off pieces of it and swallowing it. I watched and in less than ten minutes the squirrel was devoured. The Goshawk stood there for another minute or two, then took off quickly and swiftly flew away through the trees. A Goshawk is a little larger than our common pigeon. It stays mostly in the trees and mostly flies low, below the tops of the trees. It is very fast and as far as I know eats only meat. They are very pretty, mostly in shades of brown.

I sat very quiet and still and kept on the alert for movement of any kind. As is usual, in most of the woody areas, practically anywhere in these United States and Canada The little striped ground squirrels that we call chipmunks were soon coming out of their burrows in the ground and running around under the leaves and flipping their tails and chirping at me because they were not sure just what I was. A large Fox Squirrel came out of a large nest in an oak tree a hundred feet or so away from where I sat, circling it as he came down. He always circles so he can see in all directions and will not be surprised while he is on the ground hunting for nuts and roots.

Various Deer and Grazers

While I was watching the different squirrels, further away a mother deer and two little fawns walked through the trees slowly. They were out of my shooting range, but close enough that I could see them real well with the binoculars. What beautiful creatures they are. They were not so little because the white spots were beginning to disappear. They grow very fast during the first two months. They were learning, for their ears were continually moving around as they searched for new noises.

As they walked through the trees, as usual the mother was ever alert, her ears in constant movement listening all directions and every few seconds she would lift her nose to the wind to catch any scents that might be there. The fawns would mimic their mother every so often but they stayed behind her all the way. When they are born they have beautiful white spots on them. The spots were nearly gone now, just a mere color change where the spots had been. They were still beautiful and so very graceful in their movements.

Their mothers have the responsibility to teach the young deer all the sounds smells, and signals they will need to know as grown ups in the life they will lead—the different scents they must leave as they flee from something they do not like, the signals of the beautiful white tail, telling of fear, pain or whatever, the audible bleeps, coughs or snorts used to communicate with each other for warnings, or just friendly communication.

A young deer, when just born until about half grown, is called a fawn. They are quite beautiful and are light tan in color with white spots. They do not give off any scent or smell for quite a while after they are born. Which keeps the predators from discovering them. The mother leaves them in some kind of covering grass etc. and they are smart enough to know not to make any sound or movement until she comes back and tells them it is ok to move.

I have only seen two or three less than a month old, but I never went hunting or looking for them in the early spring and summer. I knew they were out there but I did not want to disturb them. I have seen several sets of twins and a few sets of triplets during my spring and summer (hunting) trips into the woods near my home. Always beautiful to see and watch.

I understand it is that way with some of the other vegetarian animals in other countries. The young, when born, do not give any scent that the predators can follow, from hiding place to hiding place. In a few days the young of these animals have the strength and learn to run as fast as their mothers. That has to be a factor in their population staying as it is. In their lives, speed is essential for survival.

There is a very large variety of deer in this world, from the smallest, to the largest and nearly all have predators to contend with. The little barking deer that I hunted (without success) in the Province of Assam as well as the large Sambar deer, were not really plentiful, and were scattered out through the jungle. Their predator was mainly the Bengal Tigers of the area they were in.

In the United States there is a large variety of wild grass or forage eaters. Moose, Elk, Pronghorn elk, caribou, white tailed deer, black tailed deer, sheep, and goats are all available for the hunter to choose from. A hunter after any of the wild creatures in any of the western states will enjoy the hunt very much. There is such a variety of beauty and fascinating things in the western states that a hunter in that area will come across the most memorable sights and places that he will never forget the experience.

There are a lot of movies, shows, postcards etc that show a lot of the beautiful places throughout the west, but not as a hunter will see them when he is walking quietly and slowly. Enjoying the little things, the flowers, the little animals that he might see and even the larger animals as he comes across them in their natural habits.

The high, plains, the low valleys, the rushing rivers, the forests of all the different evergreens, or the aspen as they change color in the fall, there is so very much to see and hear in the wilderness of the Rocky mountains that it would take a lifetime too see it all and even then you would be missing something. To stand at the base of a huge Ponderosa pine and look up, or to quietly walk along a river in Idaho. These are things never to be forgotten, once you have did them. It is unimaginable beauty and feeling as you find your way through the quiet places

As it was getting dark and I was getting hungry, after the deer had gone out of my sight and I was sure they would not hear or see me. I eased up out of my hiding spot and made my way out of the woods to my vehicle and went home, very pleased with the time well spent at something I loved.

Woodchucks and Nature in the Spring

One day as I walked along one of the fencerows toward a place I liked to sit and watch for turtles in the little creek that flowed through the property that we lived on. I saw a new mound of dirt that had been freshly dug. It was about ten or so feet out from the property line fence and that put it in our hay field. One of our horses had broken a leg when it stepped in a groundhog hole the year before. My father had told me that I was to shoot any groundhogs that dug their dens out in any of the fields that the horses would be walking in. The fence was made of split trees (called a split rail fence because it was made from lengths of wood cut to the length we wanted, They were then laid in a zigzag pattern where we wanted to have a fence. They were interlocked at each end, which held them in place. The fence was built up to a height of about three feet depending on what we were trying to keep in.

That new hole was a danger to the horses when they were in the area, so it was for me to shoot the groundhog and fill up the hole. It would do no good to fill the hole with him in it because he would just dig himself out in a few minutes. So I had to figure out where to sit to get a good shot at him when he came out to eat. Groundhogs come out to eat at all hours of the day, Depending on the weather and the time of year and food available. It was late spring. So I decided to try in the evening after school. That is one of their favorite times to eat. They eat mainly grass or clover, sometimes grain in the fall of the year or if they find some ones garden, and then they eat whatever they find. They can wreck a garden if it is a small one. They do like corn on the cob, and while it is still standing. They pull it down to eat the fresh kernels on the cob.

The next evening after school and I had did my chores. I got my little .22 rifle and walked down the fence—row till I got to a spot about two hundred feet from the hole.

I found a spot that was on the opposite side of the rail fence in one of the zigs or zags. Where I could stick the gun through between the rails and have a good shot. It was just before dusk that I saw movement and then it was just the tip of his head. Just enough so that he could see all around him. I waited, and soon he came out and stood on the mound of dirt surveying his territory. He was facing to my right and was a good target. As luck would have it, he fell into the hole when I shot, and I buried him there with the dirt he had taken from the hole. With him being buried in the hole it would stop other groundhogs from opening the hole again. It was getting dark when I returned to the house to tell Dad I had shot the groundhog.

One Saturday morning after I had performed my share of the daily chores that we were to do each day I ask my mother if it was alright if I took my 22 and went back in the woods "hunting" She nodded permission and I put on my old jacket, picked up my 22 and out the door I went. It was during the last days of April so spring was just getting started, and I have always loved the spring for going into the wooded areas around where we lived. Everything was starting out fresh for the coming summer and fall. Once out of the bright sunlight of the open areas of the fields, the change was very apparent. The ground was literally a carpet of beautiful spring beauties; at least that is what we always called them. They are a little flower, about a half an inch across with only a couple of leaves that grows in the shaded areas of the woods. White with little strips of pinkish color, they grow year after year. In many places a person cannot walk without stepping on them. All around me there were signs of new growth. The little leaf buds were beginning to show on the trees and here and there I could see some leaves of the little purple violets, which I always loved to see arrive in the spring of the year. Some times in certain areas they would literally cover the ground with beautiful purple flowers, and sometimes they would be scattered all over an area.

The woods are not nearly as quiet in the spring as they are in the fall. There is an almost continual patter of birds chasing birds etc, both high and low in the trees. Both the birds and the squirrels are building nests and even the little striped ground squirrels are running around picking up grass and little sticks to take into their burrows and build nests.

Both the squirrels and the birds seem to like the taste of the new leaf buds as they start to form the leaves. It is a fascinating little world to just sit quietly and watch. At those times, the hunt is forgotten

I located a favorite old stump and sat down on the ground with my back against the stump sat still and waited. It was only a few minutes of stillness before I saw movement in some leaves not far from me and then a little ground squirrel stood up and looked around. Of course he spotted me right away and I saw his little tail flip and he gave a loud chirp and kept flipping his tail. A signal to anything watching, that something was not right in the neighborhood. I sat and watched him for several minutes as he scampered back and forth between different small logs and trees on the ground. All the time keeping an eye on me and flipping his tail as he chirped.

He ducked back into the pile of leaves and into his underground den as I got up and headed down to the little creek that wound it's way through the woods.

I approached the stream slowly as I did not wish to scare any snakes or turtles off of their morning warming up area. Both liked to come out of the water and find a spot in the morning sun to warm up and absorb the heat. Usually on a rock or small log or something. Both the little spotted, and painted turtles are plentiful in Ohio. Almost all of the little ponds or slow moving rivers and streams, have one or the other of the two species. There are a pretty good variety of snakes also in the state of Ohio, both poisonous and non-poisonous. The green grass snake, the garter snake and the black snake seem to be the most prevalent. Occasionally we see a copperhead or a water moccasin (cottonmouth) or a timber rattler comes over from Pennsylvania. Over the last few years, there seems to be more interstate migration than there used to be, perhaps just more population and they are looking for more open space.

Up until three or four years ago I never heard of a black bear being seen here in Ohio. In the last few years there have been several sightings. The same is true of coyotes. They are more prevalent now than they have ever been.

So you see, we hunters are not killing off the live creatures of the wild. On the contrary, the money we spend for hunting licenses goes to the management and control as well as relocation of some wildlife from and over populated area to a lesser-populated area. This increases the number of overall wildlife and keeps the herds healthy.

Bison is another good example of what wildlife management can do. Wild horses are another example of what happens when control takes over. Now there hundreds of horses through out a lot of the states. More people are enjoying them than ever before. How much of the money for that comes from the purchase of hunting licenses? Where would it come from otherwise? The taxpayer?

As I walked along the bank of the stream, looking for anything that moved. I spotted a snake, but he spotted me at the same time and there was a splash as he dropped off of a small willow limb and fell into the water and disappeared.

Along with the spring beauties there is a smaller flower that appears at about the same time. We called them "Forget-me-nots". The true name, I found out much later, is "Bluet". They are usually scattered throughout the wooded areas in small patches, very small and bluish-white in color. My mother loved them so when I came upon a small patch of them I stopped and picked a small bundle of them, being careful not to crush any.

After sitting again and enjoying the antics of some more of the little striped ground squirrels, I walked slowly and circled back toward the house for lunch, enjoying every minute of walking through the many new spring beauties and signs of the new growth. A patch of "Bluets" or, as we say, "Forget-me-nots" can be seen in the color plate in the front section of this book. They bloom mostly in late April, early May, and on into the middle of May.

This year was a good one for the flowers. They started in late April and kept coming clear until nearly the first of June. The weather was perfect for the blooming of the spring flowers, not too hot or too cold. The wooded areas were very beautiful.

I walked out into the wooded area of my son's property and the ground was literally covered with flowers. A person could not walk without stepping on them; even the beautiful little Trout Lily was more numerous than any other year I can remember. They are little yellow lilies about an inch or inch and a half in size with a little brown touch in them, very beautiful. They usually grow in among the spring beauties and are about six inches in height.

Mother nature is wonderful in her placement of different things of beauty.

When a hunter walks out of a pine forest and into a swampy area he notices that the colors and type of flowers and plants change also. Different areas have different characteristics and they show in the color and arrangements of nature's wonderful displays of beauty.

Beauty ranges from the Gold that is found in the ground to the tar pits of California in her display of things to see. And a hunter can see a lot of them if he spends enough time in the woods. No one will ever see them all. The world is too vast and the variables are too many and are forever changing so there is more to come.

Protect and see Mother Nature in all her beauty, become a "Hunter".

Squirrels and Turkeys

A hunter walking through the woods in the spring of the year can see all sorts of activity. They say that in the spring of the year the young man's fancy turns to thoughts of love. The same is true of the animals and birds. They all start looking for a place to start a family. The birds look in the trees and on the ground and the animals look for hollow logs or a hole in the ground. While in the woods, I have seen several nests built in the tops of trees and on the ground. The mother rabbit digs a hole in the ground, lines it with grass, leaves and finally she pulls out some of her hair and lines the inside of the nest with it, for the newborns.

The Fox and Gray squirrels usually build the birthing nest inside of a hollow tree. After the babies are a week or so old they are then carried out, by the loose skin on their neck, to a large nest of tree branches and leaves built in the fork of one of the limbs of the tree. It is usually pretty high up in the tree. In winter these nests can be seen from any highway when driving through a wooded area nearly anywhere in most of our states.

It is from these outside nests that the young learn to run and play in the branches of the trees, and are taught to watch for enemies, including the many hawks that use them for food. The young rabbits also stay in the nest for a few days before they venture out of their nest of fur. To go out before they are a week or so old could spell death, because there are always predators watching. All of the hawk family and nearly all the Owl families will catch and eat the young. They become very proficient at running and hiding from the hawks, but a good many of the young are caught and eaten. I have sat many hours and watched as many of the young squirrels learned to climb in and around the huge oak and hickory trees. If you have ever hunted them you know how amazingly fast they can move from one side of a huge Oak to the other side and then leap from the extended limb onto the limb of another tree next to it.

Moving from tree to tree, they are an elusive target. There are dedicated Squirrel hunters that hunt them each year for food. They are all vegetable and nut eaters and their bodies are large enough to make a good meal. The meat is very tasty and a little like chicken. They are plentiful in nearly every state in the union and are in no way endangered.

The little striped ground squirrel and the mean little Red Squirrel are not hunted for food. The main reason for shooting them is for population control. They can become a very bad nuisance if the population reaches a certain level, depending on the area. In a normal area, the predators keep them under control. Many hawks and the larger snakes have them as a main diet and keep the population to an even level. They can cause a lot of damage if they find a hole in a building like a shed, barn or even a house. They can chew through wood, plaster, etc. with no trouble at all. If they can find their way into your attic, they will love it and you will find all kinds of nuts all over the attic floor.

One day during the early bow season for whitetail deer in November I met a bunch of turkeys face to face I worked my way up the side of a small hill in a forested area till I came to a spot where a large tree had been blown over and the rooted area had pulled up out of the ground on one side and left a large piece of dirt and roots. This made a good shelter, as directly behind the hole it left was a huge cluster of multi-floral rose bushes that made a good background for me to sit in front of. There was already a large amount of leaves in the hole so all I had to do was to make myself comfortable and have some kind of backrest. I moved a smaller log that was nearby over to lay along side the hole. I made myself comfortable and sat down to watch for a nice buck deer to come along and give me a nice easy shot with my Crossbow.

The usual squirrels were soon moving about and the woods were quiet. Nothing could approach from behind me, so I had only to worry about the area that was visible in front of me and to each side, roughly one hundred eighty degrees of area.

An hour or so later a couple of does, young ones I think, walked by, down the hill a ways and I watched them for as long as I could see them.

A short time later I heard a rustling in the leaves to my right. I could not see what it was without turning my head, so I just sat there and started to turn my head very slowly. The rustling became louder and when I started to hear some chirps along with the rustlings I knew it was a group of wild turkeys.

They were getting real close now and as my head turned I was looking through the camo netting over my face, directly at the heads of three large hen turkeys. They were not more than four feet away and were looking directly at me. Their heads were turning so that one eye could see me then the other eye could see me. They were not sure they should stay there so they chirped low a couple of times, turned and slowly walked back the way they had came. That was closer than I had ever been to a wild turkey in the natural environment. I will always remember the encounter. The feeling is something that is not easily forgotten, especially if you are a lover of the out of doors and nature in general.

The buck I was looking for never did show himself that day, darkness came before he did so I would have to wait for another day.

The beard on a tom turkey signifies it is a male, and sometimes grows to be a foot or more in length. For years there were no wild Turkeys in the state of Ohio, at least none that I ever heard of. Now they are very plentiful and we now have both a spring turkey hunt, and a fall hunt as well. The strutting Gobbler is a very elusive prey; they are not only hunted by humans. Bobcats, Coyotes, fox and any meat eating animal hunter will go after the turkeys. From the time they are hatched, they are prey for something. Hawks and owls kill a lot of the young in the first few weeks after they are hatched. A neighbor of mine was out one morning, trying for a spring cobbler. He had two hen decoys and was concealed, calling and waiting for a big gobbler to answer, when he noticed movement coming toward the decoys. He soon saw that it was a large coyote and it was creeping toward one of the hen decoys. When it got close enough to see him, he moved the gun and his arm. When it saw the movement it instantly recognized trouble, turned and

disappeared. It had heard him using the hen call and thought he was a live hen. The coyote is very elusive and very hard to see, let alone shoot. The hunts are very well controlled and only the Gobblers are hunted in the spring. Some areas have larger populations than others, possibly due to habitat. They are a very sharp-eyed bird and a hunter that is able to call one in is indeed a good woodsman. With the new technology, nearly a perfect imitation of a turkey call is available for the hunter to use. Even then it is hard to fool a smart Gobbler. Again, a large majority of licensed hunters come back from the hunt many times empty-handed. They still enjoyed the time spent in the woods and the hunt

Trapping and Crows

Why do we hunt? You know, that never did occur to me. I just never thought about it. In the nineteen twenties and thirties Hunting and trapping were a natural thing for a farm boy to do. Hunting and trapping were done as a necessity. Trapping brought money into the household and hunting put a lot of meat on the table. Not a lot in today's terms but at that time it was to our family, a lot.

When the trapping season came around I knew just where all the fur-bearing animals were and just where to set the traps. The money I received from the furs I sold paid for nearly all my school clothes through the sixth grade

During the summer vacation from school I spent a lot of time on hunting trips into the wooded areas around the house we lived in. The hunting season did not start until late in the fall, so I kept my shooting to killing crows that would pull the young corn shoots up and eat them. It is surprising how much corn they can destroy during the short time the corn shoots are relatively short and easy to pull up.

The black crows were so plentiful at that time that the state put bands on their legs with monetary rewards for them if you happened to shoot one with a band on it. The band was put on a leg when the young crows were in the nest. Crows have been plentiful in Ohio for decades and it was not until sometime in the nineteen eighties (I think) that they finally stopped open season on hunting them. They still have three days a week that they can be hunted. I do not hunt them and haven't for years; they are a nuisance sometimes, but not much.

I even feed them sometimes when I have leftover or stale bread. I have a large yard and I throw the slices of bread out in the yard, come back in the house and get my crow call and go back outside and give what I think is a call to food. Usually, a few minutes later the smaller crows will appear, then a little later the big cousin of the crow, the Ravens will appear and they all will clean up the slices of bread.

I do not have to call them anymore. They must be watching the house, because a few minutes after I go out and scatter the bread, doughnuts or whatever they show up in the surrounding trees and are soon carrying off slices of bread. There is not too many living and nesting in this area so they do not become noisy or overcrowding. They keep a sharp eye on my kitchen door. If my face appears there, they will fly up to the trees and wait till I back up where they cannot see me.

When you see more than one crow or raven on the ground feeding, you will nearly always be able to see another one sitting somewhere keeping a lookout for anything that is coming toward them. It will always be on a high treetop with good visibility in all directions. As a boy, I found that out real fast. When I saw the crows down in the cornfield picking on the corn shoots, I would try to get a hill or something between the crows and myself so that I could move closer without being seen. As soon as I was about to get within range of my twenty-two rifle, I heard a loud crow calling from a nearby tree with a dead limb in the to of it. I soon learned to watch for the lookout instead of the flock on the ground.

Crows and Ravens are now seen in many countries and have a variety of names. They do not seem to be much of a pest and people everywhere are familiar with them. They have been around for a long time, Edgar Allen Poe's "The Raven" tells about them and that was a long time ago. They are really harmless creatures unless they become too numerous and. Noisy. The numbers are kept down around here, I think, by the farmers' use of pesticides on their corn and fields and killing of useless grass and brush with poisons. Crows and ravens do eat dead meat off the road or dying insects that have been poisoned.

I do not trap anymore either, but there should be some trapping to keep the animals under control and stop the killing on the highways. The small black and white skunk is getting a little out of control in some areas. Along the New Jersey coast, at the edge of the wetlands, they are quite numerous. In one village that had banned trapping them, they became so destructive that the village repealed the no trapping ordinance for both the Skunks and the Muskrats, which had undermined the porches and banks along the wetlands.

Deer Population

Imagine what would happen if there was no open season for hunting the Whitetail deer here in Ohio or in Pennsylvania. Today on the news, they had a story about Detroit. It seems that the city is now so full of deer that the accident rate between automobiles and Deer has tripled in the last two years. Another city has called in special sharpshooters to thin out the herds there.

I do not understand people. Common sense will tell you that only so many of anything can only get bigger if nothing is done to control the multiplication factor. In the case of deer, if they cannot be shot, what are you going to do about them? No one wants to donate money to catch them and ship them out to another area. The city involved said they are going to shoot about six hundred of them and donate the meat to the shelters. A good idea, it sounds like to me.

Just the other day not far from here a man driving a pickup truck was killed when a deer jumped across in front of his truck. It jumped high enough that when he hit it, it was directly in front of the windshield and it went through the windshield and half way through the back window killing him instantly. There are many thousand deer killed each year, and every year the herd comes up to about the same, as it was the year before. Just imagine how many deer there would be if it weren't for the hunters. Many of the Does give birth to twins which more than doubles the number of Deer that are added each year. They have to be controlled; it is only common sense.

Thousands more are killed each year during the Bow and gun seasons. Through all this the deer population stays nearly the same.

The States Division of Natural Resources is now very good at regulating the hunting laws to keep it that way.

There were no deer in the state of Ohio when I was a child and it was not until the late nineteen thirties that I saw my first deer. Now there are Whitetail Deer in all the forty-eight states, or so I've been told.

They are fast becoming a nuisance in some of the larger cities here in Ohio. Some of the cities are starting to hold special hunts and regulations to keep the herds down.

In the lower states and some of the northern states there are large farms where deer management takes place and they regularly use the hunting season to control their deer population. Both Bucks and does are harvested to keep a healthy and controlled herd. They use food plots to see that the deer are getting the proper balance of minerals and proteins. It is profitable for the landowners and the deer.

So you see, we hunters are not "killing off all the pretty deer" or are out killing for the fun of it"

If you know your history you know that men have been fighting as far back as you can look. It is the same way in nature. When two males of the same species come together, they first look each other over. If it is to be fight, they fight. If it is to be friendly, they become friends. For centuries it has been up to the man to provide for the family. In many cases Nature has made the male the provider and the protector of the home, nest or cave, whatever. The physical and mental makeup of the male has made him the one looking for a challenge. So that is part of the reason for our hunting, it is a challenge, to see if we can outwit the prey.

That is one of the many reasons that we hunt, the challenge.

Many of us hunt with a camera. We see the beauty and we have the challenge. The ability to creep, crawl, or whatever to get close enough to anything live in nature to get a good close picture, sometimes gets very demanding and clever.

Not too much is required in today's world. With telescopic sights and cameras with zoom lens one needs no hunting skill at all to get close up shots of anything.

If you want to see or watch them at play, or to just get a close-up without being seen, you will have to resort to the hunting technique: stay hidden, move carefully and slowly, as a hunter does, and wear dark clothes. Any little movement is quickly seen. To see what I mean, just stand and look into a patch of woods for a few minutes. Look straight in, steady. Soon a bird or something will move. Notice how quickly your eyes went to the thing that moved. That is what I mean. The wild animals are even better at it than we humans. Their lives depend on how quickly they see a predator if one comes. Protect and see Mother Nature in all her beauty, become a "hunter"

One fall I put on my camo outfit and walked about a half mile back behind my house to see what I could find. It was early fall and the bow-hunting season had just started. The weather was perfect, a nice sunny day and a good day to sit somewhere and see what would walk past. There was a little stream that came down from a large tree farm, a mile or so behind my property. It made a little valley that was wooded and I had noticed deer trails crossing the area.

I entered the wooded area as quietly as I could and I had used the spray scent-blocker on my rubber-bottomed boots so that a wondering deer could not discover my trail into the woods. I had found out the hard way that even wearing rubber boots, some scent would be there where you step.

One day a year or two past I had walked into the woods wearing rubber bottomed boots and had walked directly to one of my tree stands that overlooked a good deer trail. I had to cross the deer trail to get to the tree that the stand was in. I climbed the tree and sat on the platform. About an hour later, two yearlings came along the trail. The lead doe is usually a more experienced deer and as she walked she would occasionally lower her nose and scent the trail. When she came close to the place I had crossed their trail she stopped, put her nose to the ground and then slowly stepped back, turned and slowly went back the way she had come. The other deer turned and followed her. That was a good lesson for me.

As I walked farther into the woods I started looking for a good place to sit and watch for a large Buck that I had glimpsed a few times during the summer. I came across a well-used trail that came over a low bank and went down to the stream. Off to one side of it there was a large patch of multi-floral roses. With my tree trimmers (which I usually carry) I cut a hole in the bottom layer of the branches, put my camo colored hot seat in the spot on the ground and sat down.

Where the trail came down the bank was only about three or four feet from the spot where I sat. When the trail reached level ground, it turned to the right and went directly in front of where I sat. I was only about six or eight feet from anything that would come walking along that trail.

After an hour or two I saw movement off to my right and soon a large Doe came slowly along the trail towards me. I sat very still, hardly breathing and watched as she came slowly along, Ears turning continually and her nose moving up and down as she listened, and scented the air.

As she came slowly along the trail, several times she looked directly at me but with my camo facemask down and my hands covered with camo, I blended too well with the bushes and background. She walked on and turned up the trail that went over the rise beside me. She was a beautiful animal and I had never been that close to a living deer before and I was shaking with tension and my heart was pounding, it was a wonder that she had not heard it, talk about exciting.

After she had been gone a few minutes, I flexed my muscles and stretched my arms a little then sat still again. A few minutes later I again saw movement off to my right. Gradually two three or four-month-old fawns came into view and were following the same trail that the Doe had. They were walking slowly, one following the other. They also stopped and looked directly at me, but they were just curious. One stuck his nose over toward me, but did not leave the trail. They then continued the same route that their mother (I believe) had taken, putting their noses to the footprints that the other deer had left as they followed the same trail.

They were very beautiful, with faint white spots from their earlier coloring. I've not forgotten how beautiful and how exciting they were. It was a very pleasant and memorable day. It is hard to describe the feelings that you feel when they are so new and unusual.

Spider in the Snow and 4 point Buck

One morning in western Pennsylvania that I remember so vividly was so unusual that I will never forget it.

The men and I left our cabin about an hour before daylight and were at our places where we were going to be as daylight came. It was early December and a heavy snow had covered the ground with four or five inches of the white stuff during the night. In Pennsylvania a hunter is required to wear at least one hundred square inches of hunter orange during the gun-hunting season. It appears that deer are colorblind and only see in black and white. I was dressed in an orange pair of insulated coveralls, with a hood, no less, and more clothes underneath. The temperature was around two or three degrees below zero and it was cold, very cold.

I slid down into the spot where a tree had been blown over and the roots had came out of the ground and left a large hole which had filled with leaves earlier. I moved the snow out and put my hot-seat on the leaves and sat down to await the coming of daylight.

Directly out in front of me there were a lot of young white pines about fifteen feet high. The snow had covered the limbs and branches of the trees and all the larger trees as well. Not much moved in the woods when the weather was this cold and the snow was that deep, this was really hibernating time for the creatures of the deep woods. They had nearly all carried food to their nests. Now was the time to eat scarcely and no more than one needed to survive, it may be a long winter.

The sight was beautiful as the sun came up and gradually opened them to my view. There was a slight fog in the air and the stillness was unbelievable. Little wisps of fog were drifting around in the air. It looked as if some of the air had just frozen and was floating through and around the trees. There was not a breath of wind.

As I sat there, unmoving, enjoying the feelings and sights. A little white spider, about the size of a grain of rice, slowly lowered itself down, directly in front of my face. I could not believe what I was looking at. Here, in the dead of winter was a live spider lowering itself down to the ground, to do what? Three degrees below zero and it did not seem to mind the cold.

I took my gloved hand and moved the web, above him with him on it over to another branch to my left and behind me. I do not know where he ended up. I was looking for deer.

No sound broke the beautiful silence as I sat there, unmoving, but seeing all that was in the approximately two hundred degrees of area that I could cover, by slowly moving my head a little one-way or the other.

A little later as I sat there, my eyes caught a little movement beneath the white pines that were in front of me. As they came closer, I could see that they were the feet of several deer that were walking through the young pine trees for cover. The young pine tree foliage grew a lot closer to the ground than the older trees. The deer were using them for cover as they traveled. The Deer were not exposed except for their feet and a few inches of their legs. There were six of them and they came out of the pines farther over to my left, All were Does and beautiful to watch. They never looked my way as they went on their way. I heard no sound as they went by for the snow was soft and fluffy. Later, after I head eaten a sandwich I had brought along and a chocolate bar, I saw some feet again and waited. These feet looked a little bigger and I suspected a couple of bucks. They walked slowly through the little pine trees and finally showed themselves to my left. Sure enough they were

Bucks and one was a nice four pointer with a little spike Buck following I wanted the meat for the freezer so I lined the sights of my rifle on the lower chest of the four pointer and squeezed the trigger. The shot was good and the buck dropped to the snow. My hunting day was now over and I had work to do. I performed the necessary procedure and after two hours of dragging one hundred pounds of meat for a distance of about one mile, I finally had it hanging beside the cabin to cool out. I could relax now, but I missed the quiet. For the rest of my stay in the cabin I would start about noon and walk the sides of the hills to move the deer toward the hunters. I could not carry a gun in the woods anymore this season. One winter when I was walking to move deer for the other hunters, I came across a bear track. It was a fresh track and I wondered why it was not in a den somewhere hibernating. I did not follow those tracks. As a matter of fact I walked the other way, as I had no gun with me.

Porcupine

A year later I was in the same area on opening day of the Pennsylvania Deer gun season. The snow was nearly six inches deep and it was a very still day again. I had found a large tree stump that was just the shell of the tree and the space in the center was large enough for me to sit down in it with only my head above the stump. I had my bright orange coveralls on and I had brought along an orange toboggan to put over my head. I was very warm and comfortable in my little hole in the tree stump. There were large Hemlock trees all around me and they were quite beautiful with the snow caught in the needles. From my seat I could look in all directions but behind me. About ten feet from me, directly in front of me there was a large hemlock that was hollow from the bottom up. I did not know how far up the hollow part went.

About mid-morning I heard some scratching coming from the hollow tree and then little pieces of wood began to fall from inside the tree.

I had no idea what it was, maybe a squirrel or raccoon, an opossum maybe. I watched and soon a large porcupine lowered himself, or itself, whichever, to the snow. It then turned and waddled away, down the slight slope of the hill, leaving tracks that looked like a miniature army tank had driven through the snow.

I had noticed earlier that the bark had been eaten off of the wild cherry trees in the area. The Porcupines seem to like the taste of the bark and will clear quite an area on the sides of the trees. Sometimes killing the tree as a result. I had seen a few on my fishing trips into Ontario years ago in the sixties and seventies.

Canada has lots of them and they migrated south as far down as central Pennsylvania. I have no idea where they are I haven't seen any here in Ohio yet, but they will probably make it sometime. There really aren't that many forests here in Ohio anymore.

They are nocturnal, and are rarely seen in the daytime. They stay up in the trees most of the time and climb from tree to tree, eating the buds and flowers or whatever as they travel, mostly at night. They have very short legs and have few enemies or predators. The latter due to the approximate thirty thousand very sharp quills that cover their bodies on the top and sides. When and if a predator comes close, the porky just turns his back and when the predator comes close he hits him with his tail, which is also covered with quills. The poor predator then spends the next hour or so trying to get the quills out of his nose, paw or whatever.

The larger predators just do not want to bother trying to get to the underbelly of the porcupine. There is too much risk involved for them. The quills have a way of sticking in the flesh and skin of whatever comes in contact with and is very hard to get out. Even the fierce mountain lion steers clear of the lowly porky. Their feeding and breeding range covers most of Canada and clear up to Alaska.

I had become familiar with the Porcupines while in Canada a few years before. I had not seen any in Pennsylvania before and was somewhat surprised to see this one in the middle of winter. They evidently stay up inside the hollow trees and come out to eat. Later I found several trees that were hollow and noticed a large pile of droppings at the bottom of the hollow part. There were several different areas where I saw the odd tank-like tracks and knew that the Porcupines were out eating again; a very interesting encounter again as I was "Hunting".

Later that afternoon as I sat in my hole in the stump, enjoying the quiet stillness and watching an occasional blue jay or flicker flying from tree to tree, I thought I heard the crunching of snow and the adrenalin started to build up. Soon I could see the tips of ears and then the heads of deer began to show off to my right. They were coming directly towards me and I was still as a statue, my heart pounding.

It was a large herd and I tried to count them as they walked right past the stump I was in, but I was too exited I kept perfectly quiet and just moved my eyes behind the mesh mask I had on. They were going by on each side of the stump and I was trying to enjoy the moment and look for a buck at the same time. There must have been at least twenty of them, both young and old in the herd. Some of them looked directly at me as they passed, but they were not scared. With my facemask on and only my head showing it was like a bump on the stump.

There was not enough room in the hollow stump for me to turn and watch them go, but I heard them for a few more seconds and they walked out of my range. Boy what an experience. It took me a while to calm down.

Those hills in Northwestern Pennsylvania in and around the National Forest are very beautiful and are a Deer hunter's paradise. The Hemlocks and other trees are beautiful any time of year, and one never knows what he may see or hear and it will always be beautiful or memorable.

The Oil wells came in and drilled and put in pipes and large tanks and kind of messed up some of the forest area but it did not seem to affect the Deer. Once the necessary pipes and tanks were in placed and the Deer became used to them, it was nearly the same. When I went back thee next year there were deer tracks all around the tanks and well equipment. They even became used to the pressure release valves as they released the pressure inside the huge tanks. It was a very loud noise but the deer became used to it and merely looked up as it sounded.

There are a lot of strange things that happen in nature that we humans do not understand. For example, one day I was sitting on my back porch just enjoying the day.

Bird and Animal Communication

There were two, large blue spruce in my back yard. Right behind them was a wire fence that kept the cattle out of my yard, with fence posts about every ten feet. These posts were fairly large. Measuring about six inches in diameter. There was one of them near the Blue Spruce that had a flat side on it.

As I sat there enjoying the morning, a red-bellied woodpecker came flying in and landed on the top of the post with the flat side. He sat there for a while and every once and a while I could see his bill opening and closing and every so often his tail would flip up and down. All this time his head was turning side to side and up and down with different motions. After about a minute of this, another woodpecker came flying in and landed on the same post. The first woodpecker climbed down the side of the post and stopped about a foot above the ground and hung there on the flat side of the post. Suddenly another woodpecker came, and then another, until there were a total of five red-bellied Woodpeckers on the post. I began to wonder just what was going on. There was nothing on the post that they could eat. As I watched them they all began to assemble where the first one had climbed down to and stopped, on the flat surface of the post. The next thing was somewhat amazing for they formed a circle with each of the five birds positioned like the five points of a star. All the birds were facing in, so that their heads were nearly together.

Then began a session of head moving, tail flipping and what must have been chattering, because their bills were opening and closing as if they were talking to each other.

I could not hear anything, but they must have been making sounds. (I could not near the high ranges of notes since I had worked with Jet engines a long time and my high range of sound was totally destroyed) for the books say that they do chirp etc.

That meeting went on for about four or five minutes until one of them abruptly flew off, and back to the wooded area behind my house. The others left too, a few seconds apart. The one that had come first was the last to leave. He climbed up the post, sat on the top for a while then flew back across the road to the valley he had came up out of. Those red headed woodpeckers have been back several times to the feeder I put up next to the post they had their meeting on. It is about ten feet from my back office window and I can sit and watch them as they come to eat. I never see more than one at any one time, and I cannot tell them apart so I do not know if there are more than one or not. There are a few other types of flickers and woodpeckers around here also. Some of them are meat eaters and just eat the ants etc. that crawl around and up and down the big maple trees in my yard. Between those and the Flycatchers that are nesting under my eves they consume a lot of insects.

I know that birds and animals communicate because I have seen them in the natural settings I will say more and tell you of the many times that I know there was communication and I witnessed the results.

Most, if not all of the birds and animals of the woods and fields have some means of communicating. Some flutter their wings or flip their tail. Some turn their heads or bob their heads up or down. Deer use their tails to signal to other deer. They also use vocal sounds. When walking through the woods if there is no trouble, they leave very little scent. If there is trouble or they are scared, they will leave a different scent from special glands on their legs to tell any that are following that something is wrong and to stay away or run. The scent is left on the ground with the hoof print and any animal coming behind will detect it and leave or turn around and go back the way it came.

Many a hunter has seen a good buck approaching, suddenly have it stop, look around then turn and run back the way it came. Another deer had probably seen or heard the hunter come into the wooded area and had left the scared scent as it ran out of the area.

It never ceases to amaze me how fast word travels to other birds and even to the squirrels when I refill the bird feeder in my back yard. Within minutes they are all back to it and the blue spruce beside it, waiting their turn to eat. They can hear for great distances and can see for greater distances, so there must be some kind of communication between them. The crows, in particular, can see for a long distance. The other day I took some stale bread out in the yard and scattered it around. I looked for the crows, but did not see any. I came back into the house, looked at my watch, waited a few seconds, and then looked out into the yard. I did not use the crow caller. As I watched out the kitchen window, suddenly a large crow flew into the oak tree at the edge of the yard, I looked at my watch, and it had taken only ninety seconds. It had probably seen me leave the house and watched me scatter the bread. Crows do a lot of harm to the smaller and weaker of the bird families. They love eggs and will sit in a tall tree somewhere and watch the smaller birds for a period of time. Soon they will know just where the mother bird goes most of the time after she picks up a bug, worm or whatever food she was after. The crow then knows there is a nest in that area and in the early hours of daylight the next morning it will fly into the area and find the nest, eat the eggs or young birds and leave with the mother bird chasing and diving at the crow. I have seen that happen many times during my hunting years. Crows, Blue Jays and Purple Grackles do that every year, many times. There is no way to know just how many times a pair of birds will try to raise a family before they succeed and finally have the young leave the nest. It must be very discouraging to those would be parents that are trying to start a family. Crows, Blue Jays and Purple Grackles are among the worst of the predators that prey on the smaller birds.

I live alone and I do not eat much bread. When I buy a loaf of bread I usually have a half of loaf left after a week that I have to throw away. A few years ago when this started, I took the left over bread out in the back yard and threw it so that it broke apart and scattered over the yard. I looked at it and then went back into the house and retrieved my old crow call. Back in the yard I proceeded to give the call of a crow calling to his friends, three loud caws, in two different directions. I went back in the house and sat down for a few minutes. After about half an hour I got up and went to the back door. I looked out into the back yard and sure enough there were about five crows flying in and then out of the yard. Each one was carrying a slice of bread as he left. I watched to see where they were taking the bread. All they did was fly away from the yard for a little distance and sit in a large tree and eat the bread. Some of them just flew a little ways away from the house and landed in the field behind my house and ate the bread there.

I have been doing that now for several years and they always come for whatever I put out. Lately they have been bringing their larger cousins, the Ravens along. The Ravens have been migrating down out of Canada and now there are more and more of them seen. The Ravens are or seem to be quite a bit smarter then the common crow. The ravens will figure out how to untie a knot to get something, but I have never seen a Crow do that.

My older brother has a lot of bird feeders on his back patio and several humming bird feeders. If any of the humming bird feeders become empty, the first bird to find it empty will fly to the kitchen windows, where they have often seen my brother working inside. It will then fly back and forth close to the glass till they get his attention. After he refills the syrup in the feeder they continue feeding. That is what I call real communication. They couldn't say it any plainer if they could talk. I had a humming bird feeder up one year outside my kitchen door. If I opened the door and went out and the feeder was empty, the male would fly down in front of my face, not more than ten or twelve inches away and just hover there and look at me. I would then back up into the kitchen and get the syrup I used in the feeder and then I would go back out and fill the feeder. I wear glasses and several times I wondered what he thought they were. I don't know if he could see himself in the reflection or not. A raccoon climbed up where he could grab the feeder one night and tore it down and broke it. It was the middle of the summer and I just left it down.

There is only one species of humming bird in this area, I think. They are not too plentiful and I do not like to have them become to dependent on the feeder to live. This fall when the fall flowers are dying I may put up a feeder to help them prepare for the long flight south. There is not much for them to eat that late in the season and it is a long flight.

Both the Ravens and the Crows have several different calls that they use to communicate. Their Alarm calls are easily understood, but I haven't figured out the rest of them yet.

Not all the animals and birds have alarm calls, most just run or hide until the trouble or potential trouble is gone. The alarmists are usually the birds. The White tail Deer has an alarm snort and will stamp the ground. Even the squirrels do not always sound an alarm, they just run and hide.

There are so many things that we do not know about the wildlife on this earth that make going hunting so much more interesting. A hunter never knows what to expect as he walks or quietly sneaks through the woods in search of an elusive prey.

There is danger, more in some areas of the country than others. When you are stalking a dangerous large animal, it could possibly kill you if you make a mistake. If you are after small game that will not happen, there is always pleasure though in any hunt.

The danger comes in many different forms, from the sharp points of a wild rose bush to the deadly bite of a poison snake. Nearly all of the States have a poison snake of some variety in them and the likelihood of a bite is very rare, but it could happen.

The brushing against the vines throughout the country that can cause severe itch and rash are very likely unless one is alert all the time. Poison ivy and poison oak are very prevalent and are easy to brush against if you are not careful.

Anyone going into unfamiliar area must use common sense and be careful of anything he or she is not familiar with.

During the summer and fall, there are a lot of berries and fruits that a hunter can see and eat if he so chooses. Blackberries, raspberries, strawberries etc. are readily available and are very tasty. There are other berries, thorn apples, and various nuts that can be eaten also.

If you are not familiar with what you see or find, DO NOT EAT IT. Check it out later with some one who knows what it is.

The wild strawberries have a very distinctive flavor and taste very good. The sad part is they are slowly disappearing and not being cared for, are rather small, but very tasty. A berry similar to the blackberry is the Dewberry. The vines are very low to the ground and the fruit is very good. The vines can trip you easily, so be careful walking. The dewberries are black and look just like the blackberries. They taste like the blackberries also

There is always some beauty in a flower or two that are still blooming in the fall of the year also.

Pleasant Surprise

One fall morning at the beginning of the Bow hunting season for White tail Deer. I selected my green and brown camouflage coveralls for a quiet hunt into the wooded area near my home. The leaves were still on the trees in large quantities and the underbrush was till showing green foliage. I took down my Crossbow and selected some good arrows and put in the quiver attached to the bow. Off I went, into the woods for a day of enjoying the fall season and maybe getting a good shot at a young Buck.

In the center of the wooded plot the land rose and formed a small hill about one hundred feet above the surrounding land. This made a good vantage point for a hunter to see what was going on around the area.

The wooded area was fairly large and was inhabited by a variety of birds, squirrels, skunks, woodchucks etc. The Deer had gradually worn regular paths or trails though out the wooded area. I picked a spot on the west side of the hill that had a large blackberry bush. The bush was big enough to act as a background for my body and was also within good bow range of a good trail that was well used. I knew the spot well as I had used it before and knew that there was a small stump, just inside of the longer briars that I could use as a backrest. With my pair of brush cutters that I always carried I cut away enough of the long briars to provide an opening for me to sit comfortably in.

Once in position with my facemask pulled to cover my face and glasses I relaxed and waited to see what the day would bring.

It was not long before the birds and squirrels came out and started their daily running and flying around. The morning went rather fast, and after I had ate one of the chocolate bars I had brought along to help my stomach a little, I settled down to wait out the afternoon. A few minutes later a large bird flew right past my position not more that five or six feet away. I had not heard a thing and was rather astounded when it happened. Surprised, I looked after the bird and watched it land in a large tree a few dozen feet away to my left. It was facing away from me and I could not see its face. I took out my small pair of binoculars and focused on the large bird. When they eat anything with fur on, their stomach separates the fur and rolls it in little round ball. When the balls of fur get so big, the bird throws up, and spits it out, wherever it is. They are quite beautiful and their feathers are so very soft that it is like rubbing soft thin cotton when you rub your hand over them.

As I looked at the bird through my binoculars, it turned and looked in my direction. I recognized it at once as what we called a Barn Owl. It was beautiful, with a nearly white under side and light brown wings etc with darker gray mixed over its wings and back. The white underside was sprinkled with darker light brown spots. It was what we had called a monkey-faced Owl. The large eyes were just above a long down sloping nose terminating in a hooked type beak. All that was surrounded by a dark brown ring, which gave it a monkey face look. Inside the ring was nearly all white, except for the eyes and beak. It was a very beautiful bird.

The part that so surprised me was the fact that as it flew toward me and past me I did not hear the slightest sound except for a slight swish of air. Most birds make noise when they fly, sometimes very loud.

The Owl family, I found out later after some research, do not make any noise as they fly. Their wing feathers are not the same as other species of birds. When hunting for food, they must be quiet in order to approach their prey.

They do not usually hunt in daylight, so some one or some thing probably chased it out of hiding that day. It was another surprise for another enjoyable hunting trip

That particular bird was what we normally call a Barn Owl. They like to sleep in a barn during the day. They catch a lot of mice in the barns and the farmers like to have them around. They are seldom seen, either day or night. And it was a rare sight to see one in the daylight. Oh how I wished for a camera! This was another pleasant hunting experience.

As a boy I noticed everything. At night, the sounds were always interesting to me and I would wonder what made them. In those days there were a lot more of the little Screech Owls than there are now. I began to mimic their calls and late in the evening I would go outside and stand near one of the large Maple or Oak trees that were there and I would mimic the call of the little Screech Owl. The first time I was surprised when I got an answer, and even more surprised when the second answer came from the tree over my head. I had not heard him or her fly into the tree. I was pleasantly surprised at my success at calling the little bird.

It is only from seven to ten inches tall and it can be found all over the state of Ohio and the whole of the United States. There are other Owls in Ohio. The Barred Owl and the Great Horned Owl are also plentiful. The Great horned Owl is the one we call the Hoot Owl, because his call is sort of a "hoo hoo hoo hooooooo", and you can hear it for quite a distance. The Great Horned Owl is not particular what it catches, be it cat, dog rabbit skunk, opossum or any other animal it thinks it can pick up.

The Young in Danger

During the early spring and summer there is not much to hunt. Except for the few pesky crows and the ever-digging woodchucks, there is not much to watch for. When I was young, I looked for the snakes and turtles along the streams and rivers. As an adult I mostly go into the woods to enjoy the new growths and the flowers that are associated with it. That is also the time for the birth of the young fawns and it is a rare sight indeed when you walk upon a newborn fawn. They are usually found laying quietly in a clump of grass, weeds or leafy ground. They will not move until you practically step on them. They are very beautiful and the white spots stand out against the light tan of their bodies. You can bet that when you find one of them, the mother is standing somewhere near watching your every move. If you make eye contact with the fawn it will usually get up and wobble away to another spot and curl up again on the ground

The young squirrels and woodchucks (groundhogs) are beginning to come out of their hole in the ground, or nest and go exploring. They are very interesting to watch. They will run back to the nest at the newest sound or even the falling of a leaf. Anything new to them will send them scampering. A few of them will not live very long because of the Hawks, Owls, and Bobcats and now in this area an occasional Coyote. The red Fox mother also catches a lot of the new babies in the area. They particularly like young kittens. Where the back road that I live on left the main highway, there was a large house on the corner lot. I had noticed that nearly every day as I passed the house there was a small kitten on the steps at the back door. Having been young once, I knew that a young kitten, left outside alone, will just sit there and keep meowing to get back in the house.

One day, as I was coming home from a trip into the local village for groceries, as I turned off of the local state route onto the back road that led to my house, a large red Fox crossed from the house side of the road to the field side and in it's mouth it held a small kitten. It climbed the small hill on the right side of the road and disappeared from my sight. I had seen a small girl at the house a few times and she had my sympathy. The Fox had probably heard the cat meowing to get in several times and had just waited for a chance to grab it when no one was around. An adult Fox can hear a kitten meowing for several hundred yards.

I knew there was a fox in the area for I had seen her several times while hunting. I was not interested in bothering her, as I liked to see them in the wild. The year before she had given birth to a litter of three kits. I had watched her gather field mice and young squirrels and take to the den, which was within sight of my house if I used my binoculars. I had watched her many times until the kits and her left the den and moved on.

One of the commercial calls used to call a Fox or coyote is a recording of a lost kitten, calling for its mother. It is very effective for coyotes in the western plains.

Mostly though, the red and gray foxes usually hunt the open fields and meadows for field mice that are very prevalent and are very easy for them to catch. Mice are a lot easier for the young foxes to eat.

In the areas where Bobcats are living, they take a lot of young birds and animals. Few people ever see a Bobcat before it sees them. They are very stealthy. They like canyons and dense forests with swampy areas away from humans, although some are getting quite close to human habitations, but as yet are not a problem. They live mostly on young rabbits and small animals as well as snakes and mice. Their coloring is from white to darker brown, scattered over the body so as to blend it in to the surrounding trees leaves rocks etc. Their tail is about five inches long, on a body that is nearly thirty-six inches long. Hence the name Bob cat.

In all my years of being in the woods, I have only seen a few. Then only for a moment, then it was gone. The Bobcat seems to be a lot smarter than many of the other wild things I have seen and heard of only one case of a Bobcat being killed or hit on any road or highway. And the wildlife people say they are more numerous that ever before in most areas. There are very, very few ever seen. This all means that they are a thinking animal and even seem able to use common sense and estimate speed and distance, in the case of highway crossing, and knowing to keep out of sight of the human population.

There are many other animals that can be seen while hunting, if you are very careful and keep alert. The variety changes as you travel across the country. Each one has it's own particular beauty. When you see one, it will be something you will remember always.

Antique Animal—Opossum

The one animal that always stays the same is the Opossum. It seems that they have remained the same since the Dinosaurs were here. They give birth to five, six, or seven young every spring and carry them on their backs with the young ones hanging onto their mother's tail, which she conveniently curls up over her back for them to hang on to. They are the only animals with their brain in their body instead of their head like everything else. When trappers used to hit them over the head to kill them, then lay them aside to skin later. When they came back later to remove the skin, the animal would be gone. They had not killed the animal, but had just bruised it. It had played "possum" till the man had left it alone, then had just got up and walked away. I was a Taxidermist for a while and I was asked to make a mount with a large Opossum. To make the head right, I had to remove the skull and clean it in order to preserve it with arsenic. As I was cleaning the meat out of the eye sockets and around the skull I found out that the top of their head is like the breast of a chicken, just a vertical thin bone with meat on both sides of it. The Brain is down behind the front legs where it is protected.

One year I met a friend of mine and we drove to a friend's house in West Virginia to hunt for a good buck. My friend wanted to try to get a large trophy buck. He wanted to get the meat, but he also wanted to get a large set of antlers if he could. We left the house pretty well bundled up because of the twenty-two degree weather. The area was very hilly and very hard to climb if you got off of a traveled road.

We followed an old logging road to a spot about half a mile from the friends' house. The old road was fairly level as it followed the hillside about half way up the side of the hill. I positioned myself at the base of a large tree that had been too rotted to take for lumber. It was about twenty feet off of the road and would make a nice place to watch the road. There was another stump next to it and there were some small bushes and briars around that area. I cut a couple of bushes and made myself a nice place to sit so that I could see on around the hillside where the old logging road went. I was a good spot. There were some fresh deer tracks on the road and a couple off trails coming down off the top of the hill.

I did not see much movement, due to the cold I suspect. It was the first cold spell of the season and everything seems to stop. The birds were not moving and I was starting to doze off when I seen a movement where the road came around the hill and came toward me. Instantly alert, I watched. A smaller animal of some kind was coming along the road. As I watched, a beautiful red Fox came into view. It was sort of trotting along the old road, not seeming to be worried about anything.

It was beautiful, a bright white tip on it's tail and white chest from under it's nose to it's stomach. There was white on the inner side of it's ears and there was black trim around its ears and on the back of them It's feet looked back and the front legs were black about half way up. The rest of his body was a beautiful shade of red. It was a beautiful sight to see and I sat very still and watched as he came on along the road. There was not much breeze and nothing bothered him till he was just below me on the road, then he suddenly stopped and looked at the spot where I was. I did not move a muscle, I probably did not even breathe. He stood there a moment and then quickly turned and trotted back the away he had come. He evidently was not sure what was ahead, and he knew where he had come from.

Talk about excited, my heart was pounding and finally began to settle down. It was the first time I had been that close to a red fox in the wild and he had been very beautiful. In his prime and a young male.

About two hours later, in the afternoon I heard a shot down in the bottoms and I later found out that my friend had seen a large buck with a beautiful set of antlers and had made a clean shot. I helped him field dress and drag the huge animal out of the woods to his truck. As for me, it was still a beautiful day in the woods.

I am sure that no matter where a person goes in this country there will always be something that he can see that will be new to him. He does not have to be a hunter to see the grandeur and beauty of things along the way as he goes.

A few years ago I traveled out to the southern California area to visit my son who lived just outside of Palmdale. I had not ever been to that area before and it was new for me. It was the Mojave Desert. One day he said he wanted to show me the desert. We drove to and old deserted gold mining camp.

As we walked out along a dry creek bed and talked, I was amazed at the different rocks, small bushes and colored small stones in the dry bed of the creek. We climbed a small hill that seemed to be all sand. I kept slipping back one step every time I took two steps, or so it seemed. When we finally got to the top of the hill, the view was amazing. There were more hills to the north, but to the south there was nothing but flat desert.

We then walked toward the hills to the north and as we climbed upward the size of the rocks changed and they became larger. We stopped on a level area and as I stood there looking around, I was surprised to see a small bird with big eyes looking up at me from beside a large rock that was beside the trail we had came up. It was about eight or ten inches in height and stood like a statue, not moving a feather. I recognized it as one of the small desert Owls that I had seen in the wildlife book I had at home. If I am not mistaken it was a Burrowing Owl. It appears they nest in prairie Dog holes.

I am sure that many a hunter was pleasantly surprised when he was on a hunt to walk up and stop to look around and he happened to glance down and there was one of the little birds looking at him.

Any hike or walking trip into the natural areas of this country will come up with at least one surprise or another. I really enjoyed the walk that day. I had never thought about how the desert would look. It has a beauty that is hard to describe. The wildlife is a lot more prevalent than you could imagine, by just looking at the sand and Cactus. Under the surface of the desert there are a large variety of roots and seeds that are waiting to spring to life, if it ever rains. When it does rain it changes the whole view. I want to go back some day and spend a lot more time "hunting".

I also found out that it is very interesting to walk up the dry riverbeds and look at the different rocks and stones. There seems to be a large variety of them. Some are very beautiful, and of course there is always the chance of gold in that area of California. Like I said, I would like to go back sometime and spend a lot more hiking or hunting as the case may be. It is desert, but it is very beautiful and seems to beckon you when you look at it.

Trophy Buck Surprise

One day I was taking some papers to my older brother and my daughter wanted to go along. When we got there I decided I would like to take a short walk into the wooded area and check for activity by the local deer population. My daughter wanted to go along, so I asked her to be quiet and do as she was told. I told her that if she did that maybe we could see some of the animals that lived there. She said that she would do whatever I asked her to do.

She had a white blouse on, so I asked her to put on a darker color sweater that she had brought along. I was dressed in darker clothes so I would not be so easy to see. We walked back along a roadway that led to the edge of the pinewoods that covered about half of his property. We entered the wooded area slowly and I asked her to walk as quietly as she could and to be careful not to step on any sticks or tree limbs that would crack and make noise.

The wooded area was on the side of a large hill that went for a quarter of a mile or more up and over the hilltop. The bottom half of the hill was covered with a variety of pine and evergreen trees and they were planted very close together so that it was very hard to walk between them. They were all sizes, but most were from ten to twenty feet high and very dense.

We were walking along parallel to the top edge of the pine trees and were not making any noise, barely whispering to communicate. We had seen a few squirrels, but nothing else. Suddenly my daughter whispered, just loud enough for me to hear," Dad, a Deer". We both froze and I looked ahead to see where it was. Down the hill at the edge of the pines, in a little ravine that was there, stood a large buck deer. He had heard us and stopped. We had stopped first and as we were not moving, he was not sure what we were. It was a large Buck and had a huge rack of antlers. I tried to count them but the way he was standing I could not be sure. There were at least eight and probably ten, points that I could see.

My daughter and I stood as still as we could for as excited as we were. The buck watched us for a few seconds, evidently thought we were not a problem, walked on up the side of the ravine and on in the direction we had been going. It never looked back and we stood there, fascinated by the size and beauty of the big Buck. It had been only about fifty feet away from us when my daughter had seen it coming out of the pine trees and whispered to me. We had evidently stopped before it had heard or seen us.

That kind of experience does not happen often, but when it does, you will remember it the rest of your life. My daughter still mentions it every once in a while with fond memories. If we did not see another thing, it would still be well worth the time we would spend in the woods.

"I'm going hunting for a while". How many times have the urban and country living housewives heard their husbands or sons say that? In most of the cases they probably mean it. In others they may just want some time to themselves and they know that out there in the woods or wherever they go, it will be peaceful and quiet and they can relax, sit down and think things out for themselves.

If you have ever walked through an evergreen forest that was so thick that the sun never made it to the ground, and you were walking on a carpet of pine needles that were as soft as goose down. If there was no breeze blowing, it would be so quiet you could practically hear a pin drop. The lower branches of the trees, never seeing the sun, are practically bare, except at the outer tips, which do see the sun for a little bit each day. It is an awesome feeling. There is very little animal life in these trees, except at the outer edge of the evergreen area. There the squirrels come for the pine nuts and fresh tips. They seldom venture on into the center of the evergreens. They cannot see far enough to see the natural predators in time to escape with their lives.

If you are "Hunting" in hilly country you will come to open areas near or on top of the hill that will give you a beautiful view out over the valley you just climbed up out of. Each new time you look out over the valley you will see something that you did not see the last time you looked. It may be a new dead treetop where there was a new winged predator sitting. Looking out over his domain to see what he could catch for lunch. It may be a new field of grain, some farmer planted in a new location. If it is in the fall of the year it will be a panorama of beauty when the leaves turn color as they die slowly and fall to the ground. There will always be something new and as always, something beautiful to look at.

There is such a wonderful feeling, just sitting or standing there and looking at such beauty that it leaves you reluctant to turn and walk away. The feeling is very hard to describe. I do not think I have ever heard anyone describe it correctly. Several have came close, but there is too much to put into the description.

In the western states, where a hunter will walk several miles to try to get within shooting range of a trophy buck, he will stop several times to look at the terrain. He will be on alert for the trophy, but he will see the beauty of the land as he goes. Just being in those surroundings, gives him pleasure that he loves and will always remember.

As he climbs higher and higher he will notice the cold and he will risk a broken leg or a bad fall as he climbs over sharp rocks and deep crevasses. All of this is part of the "Hunt" but it is all part of why we go hunting. Many hunters have been close to death on their hunting trips, but they take it all in stride and look forward to the next time they can go on another hunting trip out west, up north or whichever direction they are going to be hunting. The pleasure is always there and it outweighs the risk many times.

Danger

Death is often very close. A timber rattler can lie quiet and suddenly strike in a vital place before you expect it. There are poisonous snakes in nearly all of the United States, I think, I am not sure about Alaska, I have never been there. I used to daydream about going there but I never made it and I probably never will.

A slip on the side of a steep hill or mountain will end in death or serious injury. In bear country there have been people killed because they surprised a large mother bear and her cubs. Every year or so someone is attacked by a grizzly and killed or injured.

If you are going to be hunting or just hiking in strange territory, you should read up on the area and study, both the beauty and the hazards so that you will be on the alert for things that might and could happen. Even the little wild pigs in Florida and some other states can do bodily harm and even kill a human if they are cornered and forced to fight. Nearly everything will fight if cornered. Even a female deer, if cornered will strike out and can do a lot of damage with her hoofs.

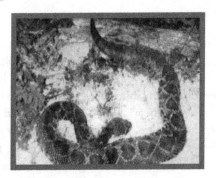

A hunter must be ever alert and be prepared to do whatever is necessary to protect himself in any situation that could come up. There is no substitute for good old common sense in any situation.

Just the other day, there was a news Item that told about a young lady biker that was attacked by a mountain lion in California. I could have predicted it. If I am not mistaken a few years ago they passed a low stopping the hunting of both Black Bears and Mountain lions. That means that the number of those two animals in the state of California will increase. It also means that the number of attacks on humans will increase, you can bet on it. There are probably cases now of bears coming into the suburbs getting into garbage cans and back yards. It will not be long before they collide with humans. Catching them and taking them far away will only help so long, then what?

Safety in the woods should be of prime concern to everybody. In snake country you must wear the proper protection from the knees down and be careful about where you sit and where you put your hands. A snake is very hard to see when it is lying still. If it is moving then you will probably see it. You can bet it has already seen you and is running away. If it is lying still, it has probably already seen you and is hoping you will walk right on by. But if you don't, you can bet it is ready to strike the minute you are within range.

A poisonous snake, whatever the kind, can blend in to it's surroundings so very well you have to be alert for a shape lying still, not something moving. When it moves it will be very fast and you must be faster. They come in all sizes and colors, so be alert.

Snow on the Mountain

One morning I left the hunting camp in northwestern Pennsylvania just before daylight. It had snowed during the night and I dressed warm and put on my lined boots for the trip across the little frozen creek and up the side of the mountain to the spot I was going to sit in for the next three or four hours. To get there I had to walk about a hundred yards to the base of the mountain, then climb up the side of it for another hundred yards or so before it leveled off for a few yards, then started up again. Where it leveled off, I turned right and walked around the mountain about half a mile. The half a mile was not level, but it went up gradually instead of steeply.

I was walking through snow about six or seven inches deep, but it was soft and fluffy and not too hard to walk through. The temperature was about nine or ten degrees above zero I was wearing my red-flannels and a regular set of clothes over them, then over all that was a pair of heavy coveralls with a hood. The coveralls were bright orange. They tell us that the deer are colorblind and cannot tell the difference. It appears that they are right. I have had a lot of Deer look at me in those coveralls and I know that they saw me, but as I was not moving, they did not think I was something to fear.

I found my favorite place where a large tree had been blown over and the hole it made in the ground where the roots had been pulled up on the side opposite the way the tree had fallen, provided me with a nice hole in the ground. I cleaned out the snow and leaves down to where it was relatively dry. Then I put my hot seat (a hot seat is a plastic covered chemical mixture in a bag about as big as a seat cushion and like a pillow, that gets warm as you sit on it) in the bottom of the hole. From the hole I could see down the side of the mountain and to my right and left. My head was about all that was sticking up out of the hole from ground level. It was a nice spot and I liked it.

From where I sat I could see down the hillside and up the other side of the valley. The other side of the valley was out of what I considered my shooting range. I do not like taking shots I cannot be relatively sure of.

About an hour after daylight came. I saw movement off to my right and soon a large buck came into view on the other side of the valley. It was out of my range so I just sat and watched as the buck climbed gradually up the mountainside. Climbing from my right to my left, it was in no hurry as it went along the side of the mountain. Finally it came to a large deadfall where it stopped.

It stood there for a while, looking all around. The deadfall was a large tree with a lot of limbs and branches and thick near the trunk. After it had made sure there was no hunter in sight, it crept into the branches of the tree and clear into the center near the trunk and I could not see it any more. Even when I took out my binoculars and tried, I could see no sign of the buck, it was well hidden.

It began to snow an hour or so after the buck had entered the limbs of the deadfall and within an hour or so there were no tracks available for a hunter to see. I never did see the buck leave, if it did. It snowed pretty heavy for a while. At about two o'clock in the afternoon, three doe came along the side of the hill below me but no more bucks came along within my vision. I heard a couple of shots on the backside of the hill I was on but nothing came by. When it became late, just before dusk. I left the hole in the ground, stretched and started back toward the camp at the bottom of the hill. About half way around the hill to where it started steeply down I passed a group of four trees that were close together. In the center of the trees on the ground, there was something brown, and as I looked closer, I could see that it was a small Doe. It did not move, but kept watching me as I came down the trail. It was not far off the trail, possibly fifty feet or so. I could sense, rather than see, that it must be hurt, possibly shot; I did not have a doe permit so I did not stop to see it. I kept walking and left it alone. I hoped it would be all right. I did not tell any one else about it. I went on back to the warm cabin at the bottom of the hill and a hot meal.

With the coming of the snow, there is a small change in the way you must hunt. The snow on the ground makes it a lot easier for the Deer to see you as you move through the trees. Likewise it is a lot easier for you to see the deer and for a greater distance. With a white background, a hunter can see any little movement, but so can the deer. The difference is in the distance, for both the deer and the hunter.

Of course, after a day or two with the ground covered, there will be telltale tracks on the ground that will show the movement of the deer and all the other animals that were out looking for food or shelter. Occasionally I have come across Bear tracks in the snow when hunting in western Pennsylvania, usually in late fall, before the hibernation started.

There were the deer tracks, along with the Porcupine, Fox, Opossum, lots off Squirrel, and occasionally a Bobcat. It is amazing how many tracks one animal can make. Once in a while the tracks of a Lynx, Mink, Skunk, maybe a Wildcat, but they are not plentiful as far as I know. I did not live there year round so I am going by hearsay. That is not too accurate in most cases.

Nearly all of the smaller animals are in their dens or nests where it is warm during the day, unless it is the squirrels. They sometimes venture out during the day, but they have a supply of food hidden in the trees and buried in the ground close to where they nest for the cold weather. So there is not too much to see during the snow covered periods, especially if the cold is severe. Surprisingly, you will still probably see something, if it is only a bird or perhaps a small spider.

Burma Experience

There are many dangers for a hunter to encounter in pursuit of his favorite pastime, more in some areas of the world than others, everything from the common cold, to being eaten alive by a Lion. Of course those are the extremes. Few people die of the common cold and very few people are eaten by a lion, in between are snakebites, spider bites, attacks by bears. Mountain lions, and any one of hundreds of things that could happen while you are in the woods, jungles, deserts, mountains and waters of the world.

When a hunter is in a new or strange place and he is not familiar with the wildlife or the terrain, he must always expect the unexpected, and be ready to handle it. Whatever it might be, as best he can.

If he happens to be hunting in a well-inhabited area he is familiar with. There should not be much of a problem. The animals that would be dangerous are probably all gone from the area and only the smaller of them remain, and would not be much trouble.

On the other hand, if he is going to hunt in the jungles of South America, Africa, Burma, or even the deep forests of Northwestern Canada, and many other places around the world, he must be ever alert.

A few years back I had a chance to do a little hunting in the foothills of the Himalayan Mountains near the province of Assam. Those mountains are covered with very dense jungle growth, both in the air for up to two hundred feet above the ground and on the ground itself. The undergrowth is everything from simple Ferns to new trees that will someday reach one or two hundred feet in height. A hunter cannot see but a few feet ahead of himself on the trail. Once he is inside the jungle and walking on the trail, he must watch where he is stepping and also the surrounding area for anything moving or hiding along the trail.

At that latitude, the trees do not shed their leaves all at once and there is a continuous falling of leaves, which means that there is a steady noise of leaves falling, day and night. A hunter must learn to distinguish one sound from another. He must learn to recognize the sounds that are no danger, from those that are or might be dangerous.

A tiger, lying along the trail for a young deer will not make any sound, so he must be watching and ready for any sudden movement. The natives that inhabit the area and use the trails regular, have cleared the trails of hiding places. They also do not travel alone, and when they do travel the areas of possible tiger attacks, they make a lot of noise by talking loud or singing. Both will let the tiger know that there are too many for him and he will let them pass without showing himself. There were very few tiger attacks on humans at that time. The jungle is too full of monkeys, Deer and fowls of different varieties for a tiger to go hungry, or attack a human.

When I first went into the jungles of Assam, I was to report to a station about fifteen miles into the jungle. I had three porters, one native boy and two native girls. All three were from one of the two villages we were to go through and knew the area well. The girls carried my personal things and the boy was to be my gun bearer. A lorrie (truck) took us to the base of the hills where the footpath started and dropped us off. Then we were on our own.

Needless to say I was as excited as a teenage boy with his first motorcycle. The first thing I found out was that walking up hill, even slowly, you do not need many clothes on. It is easy to work up a sweat the first few miles.

Back to the hunting part: I did not see much on the way in to the post. All the animals and birds could hear us coming for miles, and got out of our way. At one point along the trail we heard a tribe of monkeys howling and chattering on the other side of the valley, across from the side of the hill we were walking on. They were in the trees and we could not see them. Toward evening we came to the first village and stopped for the night. I had a meal of canned stew and relaxed and learned about the village people and some of their customs.

For the last mile or so before we reached the village, my feet had felt like they were wet. I thought it might be from my sweating. When I took my shoes off to relax for the night I found out that my socks were bloody and the bearers laughed when I looked in my shoes and dumped out a leech, fat with my blood. I had not been aware of it during the trip. They told me that below a certain altitude there were leeches all the time. They showed me what they do to keep the leeches off of them. They really don't keep them off, they just carry along a little bamboo cup with salt water in it and the leeches do not like the salt water. When it touches them, they just drop off and wait for another blood carrier. It is a funny thing, but I did not feel them when they stuck on me. I did not feel the bite at all, unless it was on a very sensitive area. As soon as they were full of blood, they just dropped off. They can slip through loose knitted clothes, like socks and they can go right through the lace holes in your shoes. If you step on one, it will cling to the sole of your shoe and then climb around and up the side of the shoe and through the cloth onto your skin and start drinking. When they attach to your skin, they inject a fluid into the bites that will let the blood flow out of your body. When they drop off after they are full of blood, the bite area will keep bleeding for several minutes; that was the reason for the wet socks. Several times while I was there I could actually pour liquid blood out of my shoes when I stopped after several miles of walking.

There does not seem to be any disease carrying with leeches. While there I did not hear of any transmission of any kind.

After eating some canned fruit and some crackers, we were ready to leave the next morning. The mosquitoes were not out yet, and we were too high now for the leeches so we were looking forward for a nice day of walking. It would take all day for the second and last leg of the trip.

A little bit about the natives that live in this area: They are called Nagas, and the surrounding area is called "The Naga Hills". There are several villages in the area, but it is a large area, several hundred square miles. The villages are pretty far apart and each village controls a certain amount of area and owns all the animal life in that particular area. The men do not wear any clothes at all unless it is raining. They have a bamboo belt that they put around their waist and carry their machete with. The girls and women wear skirts and blouses if they are in the villages within a day walk of the lowlands and the flatland people of India. Further back in the hills or mountains, if there are no strangers around, the women do not wear any top at all, just a wide strip of cloth between their legs and then brought up over a belt in the front and back. The women do all the manual labor, like cutting down all the trees in an area and clearing it to plant rice. The men are expected to do the hunting and communicating with the lowlanders.

My hunting trips, which I was looking forward to, did not happen until a week later after my official duties were completed and I had some time off. One morning I asked one of the native boys if he would like to go hunting with me. Of course he said yes and I grabbed my rifle and away we went.

I was not afraid of getting lost, but I did want someone else around if any thing happened, like a broken leg or something. We stayed on one of the main trails for quite a ways when he suggested we leave the main trail and hunt down in one of the valleys. After we had left the main trail we quieted down, no talking and no noise. When we reached the valley bottom, there was a small stream. We decided to walk up the stream and see if we could find any sign of any kind that would indicate movement of animals.

Occasionally I caught sight of movement in the treetops and was looking for some kind of squirrel. The trees were so high that it was hard to see anything. The top of the trees were so thick with leaves that no sun came through and if a squirrel did show itself it would be for a second or two at the most. Not at all what I was used to in the states. We changed our approach a little and began to move slowly and keep our eyes on what was ahead of us. Something moved on one of the large tree trunks and we stopped and stood very still and just watched. In a few minutes, at the bottom of the tree we saw a large squirrel, and I do mean large. It was about the size of one of our woodchucks, or groundhogs (if you prefer). I was amazed. We stood there quietly, not moving a hair and watched as the big animal climbed the side of the huge tree and stood on the first limb he came to and looked around. There were no limbs on the lower half of the huge tree. They did not start until more than fifty feet up the trunk.

The huge squirrel sat on the limb and looked around for a few seconds, then to my amazement, jumped straight out, opened his legs like one of our flying squirrels and like a glider, flew down to the bottom of another tree on our side of the creek, made a quick up turn and landed smoothly on the side of the tree and then quickly went up that tree, circling as it went. It disappeared into the foliage at the top of the tree. It all happened so quickly, I never once thought about my gun to shoot. It had not held still long enough for a clean shot anyway. The village people would have been glad if I had shot it for they do not get much meat.

It was nearing time to turn back toward camp, so we crossed the ridge and started back toward the campsite. Still moving quietly, we saw movement in the trees ahead. We slowed our pace and crept forward, watching for anything that would show us what was making the disturbance. Soon we caught site of a monkey. We now knew that there was a tribe of monkeys ahead. There were some big fern type leaves nearby so we huddled under them and watched the monkeys. They seemed too be moving our direction, so we just sat there and waited. It took a few minutes, but soon they were all about us, only higher up. We could see all sizes and some were carrying babies on their stomach. I thought that was a weird way to carry them but all of the young were hanging on the underside of their mothers, as they moved through the trees. I asked the native boy if he wanted me to shoot one for him, but he signaled no. I found out later that the local government permits them to shoot so many each month or whatever. One man in the village is permitted to have a gun and the local official rations the ammunition.

The monkeys played around in the trees and slowly moved on up the side of the hill and then over the top. They were chattering and making a lot of noise as they went on their way. We saw a few of them looking down, trying to see what was under the ferns, but we kept still and let them go on their way. Boy what an experience for a person who had never saw anything like that before. When they were so close I could see that they were the type of monkey that we see here in the zoos and is called Rhesus Monkey. They were all one color and are very plentiful in the cities and town in India, a terrible nuisance in my estimation.

On the way back we came to a fairly level place just off of the main trail. The boy wanted to stop for some reason. When I stopped, he walked around on both sides of the trail and was looking up into the lower branches. Every once in a while he would stop and get something off of the branches. When he came back, he showed me three small birds he had taken off of the branches. I asked him how he had caught them. He took me out to some of the branches. It seems they cut long poles, put some kind of very strong glue on the top half. Then they stick them in the ground like a normal tree. When the little birds cross the ridge. They stop to rest and when they land on the pole they are stuck. When they flap their wings to get off, the feathers get stuck too, and they are caught. We learn something new every day. Not much meat, but it is meat.

The next day, we packed enough food for a couple of days. We took along a lot of rice Two or three pounds of rice will make several meals when you add a little of my canned meat and add a little curry powder for flavor. The curry was new for me and I was a little cautious at first, but I soon came to like it, if the right amount was added to the rice sauce. One blanket was all that we needed for the nights. We were at the right level on the side of the mountain so that the temperature did not get too cold at night. The mosquitoes do not go up the side of the mountains either. Like the leeches, they were only found below a certain altitude level. We took along some salt water and also some insect repellent in the event that we would go into the valleys.

The native told me that his name was "Jim", when I had asked him what his name was. I told him I did not believe him. He just told me that it was easier for us Americans to say. "Jim" told me about a place a few miles away that resembled level ground and that there were lots of animals there.

I said, "Let's go." and away we went. There was a trail of sorts most of the way, so we made our way, keeping on the alert for anything that might show up, unexpectedly, or otherwise. I was fast becoming accustomed to the constant noise of the Jungle, and I soon learned where to look and be ready for anything that would show itself in the treetops, or on the ground. Along with that I had to watch where I put my shoes down. Sometimes the trail became quite rough, with roots, stones etc. A few times the trail became quite steep; we had to pull ourselves up the path, grabbing the young trees along side the trail and climbing. After an hour or so, the ground started to level off and we became more alert and quieter. We were climbing over the last little rise, just below a huge boulder when we heard a louder rustling ahead of us on the level area. I was in the lead and had my rifle in one hand and using my other hand to pull myself along as we rounded the huge boulder.

Suddenly, we heard a loud bellow, not real loud, but like a young calf would make calling for its mother. We found out later that that was exactly what it was. There, not more than twenty feet ahead of us was a young Indian Water buffalo and it's mother. About that time the mother also let out a bellow that could be heard for a long way. She ran up beside her calf and both of them turned and ran away from us.

We climbed on up beside the boulder and looked after them. Coming toward us and building up speed as it came was a huge buffalo bull, horns laid back and nose up, straight out. Jim hollered to me and jumped for the boulder. One side of the boulder was rougher that the others and Jim and I made it up that side of the boulder just as the bull reached it. He paced around it snorting and then paced back and forth, snorting all the time and glaring at us. It looked, for a while, like he might try to climb the rock that we were on, but all he did was walk around it snorting every once in a while and glaring up at us. Boy, was I ever glad that the boulder was there. A charging bull Buffalo is no laughing matter. They have killed hunters in Africa and India. I had started to raise my rifle when I saw the bull coming and Jim had stopped me. He told me later that several different villages own the small herds of Buffalo jointly, and that they can only kill one with permission of the local British official. The cry of the Buffalo calf and its mother had brought the bull to defend them.

We had to wait nearly an hour for the bull to finally turn and go after the rest of the herd He had wandered several feet away from the boulder, but he had kept looking back at us waiting for us to get down off of the rock. We stayed on the rock another half hour before we finally climbed down and went in the opposite direction to finish our hunting.

On the way back to our camp, I was watching the upper sections and limbs of the trees to see if I could see any new types of squirrels. We were going down the side of one of the little mountains and it was a gradual descent. The way we were going down we were able to look almost straight ahead into the tops of the trees we were coming. I caught a movement of something in the top of one of the trees and stopped immediately and so did Jim. We stood perfectly still and waited. After about a minute, I caught the movement of something moving outward on a limb of a large tree directly ahead and just a little above eye level. It was about two hundred feet ahead of where we were. When it came to a spot where I had an opening I could see through, I saw that it was a large squirrel, Jet black on it's back and the underside from it's nose back between its front legs to it's tail was a dark yellow with a kind of orange mix. It appeared to be just a little larger than our Fox squirrels back in the states. It was quite beautiful. A second later it ran on out the limb and jumped into the next tree and disappeared. I never saw another one during the time I was there. I will never forget that squirrel it was surely a beautiful animal. We arrived late at camp, tired but quite satisfied with the day's happenings. I asked Jim about the squirrel and if he had seen any. His reply was that he had only seen a couple of them in his lifetime, so they must be very secretive or very rare. They may never leave the upper terrace of tree limbs and go to the ground level. They have everything they need right there in the trees. There are nuts, buds, fruits and even water when they need it. When it rains, the water fills the cups that form at the base of the limbs where they leave the trunk of the tree. The squirrels know where the bigger cups are and use them. Of course the leaves catch water when it rains and in the morning when the dew and hot warm air is rising out of the valleys, the leaves catch a lot of moisture.

There is one thing in those hills that I really hate. It is a large yellow and black spider. They have a habit of stringing their webs across the trails just about chest high, then the spider just hangs there in the center of the trail, in the middle of the web, waiting for something to run into it. During the hunting trips, I wore only a pair of khaki shorts and my shoes and socks. The only other apparel was a large wide brimmed hat, like a Mexican Sombrero. It kept the rain out of my eyes during the monsoon season, which lasted for about four or five months. During that time there was a continual light rain and it soaked everything. During my hunting trips I was continually looking up into the trees so you can imagine how many of those spiders I ran into and most of the time they ended up on my chest, right in the center of it, web and all. I was never bitten, but I hate those things. They were about two and a half inches overall and bright yellow with black bodies and black legs. The bodies were about the size of a penny and the legs made up the rest. I found them on all the trails I traveled. Usually my right hand flipped them off faster than Wild Bill could draw a gun.

A couple of nights later at about ten thirty at night, there was a loud crashing in the brush and trees up the mountain from our tents. As we listened the noise became louder and louder until it was relatively close to our encampment. Suddenly it became very quiet. For about five or ten minutes all was quiet. Then the brush breaking and noise started again. Whatever was making the noise turned and went out around our encampment and then continued on down the mountainside. We could hear it breathing as it went, still breaking small trees and trampling brush.

We knew it was a large animal, but we were not sure if it was a water Buffalo or an elephant, so we asked Jim. He said it was an Elephant and it probably had a toothache. He told us that they always try to run away from a toothache no matter when they get it. I did not know that they could see at night but it seems it can. Of course, they do not have to be afraid of running into anything, because they are the largest animals in the jungle so they fear nothing. There are some pretty big trees there though, so they must be able to see a little.

The next morning I took my gun and Jim and went out to see what kind of tracks I could find coming down the mountain and going on down into the valley. Sure enough when we came to the area the noise had came from there were the footprints of a very large Elephant. In a spot where the ground was clear and a little soft there were some large footprints. They were so large that I could stand in one of them with both of my hunting boots on and my heels and toes would not touch the outer circumference of the foot print, that was made by a large foot!

I decided to follow the trail. I did not plan on trying to shoot an animal as large as that one with the little caliber weapon I was carrying, but I wanted to try to get a look at it. As we walked slowly, following the trail, which was very easy to follow, it suddenly dawned on me just where I was and what I was doing. I had dreamed about hunting in the jungle, and here I was, in the middle of the Asian Jungle and trailing a huge wild Elephant, to me it was nearly unbelievable.

The side of the mountain became rather steep, and I wondered how anything as big as this Elephant could navigate such hillside. About half a mile from our camp we suddenly came upon an unusual sight. The Elephant had been moving pretty fast, for an elephant, and he had suddenly stepped on a soft spot where there was a small spring on the side of the hill. The surface of the hillside had been pushed downhill from the wet spot and had finally stopped about ten or twelve feet below the spring. The weight of the huge animal had caused it to slide on the soft dirt. There was clean fresh water running out of the hillside and down across the area below where it had came out of. About ten feet of the area below the spring was a dull Black. I knew it immediately; it was a ten-foot vein of coal, solid and all pure coal. If that vein went all the way through this mountain to the other side there were millions of tons of coal there. If all these mountains had that vein under them, there was enough coal to last the world quite a while.

We never did catch up with the Elephant; we followed his trail for over a mile and then turned around and followed the valley back toward the camp. At one spot in the valley we again came across a tribe of monkeys that were feeding in some trees a little way up the other side of the valley. We left them alone and went back to camp.

One thing I was beginning to notice: There were not many birds around. I saw very few. I could not figure that out, unless the natives had caught a lot of them on the glue poles they used on the ridges. The ones I did see the most were the black Hornbills. They are a beautiful bird with their black feathers and ivory yellow bills. They stayed in the upper branches of the huge trees all the time and we had to be very careful if we wanted to get close to them. Jim told me that they mate for life and the pairs are always together. He had never seen any young ones, so they are very secretive in their nesting.

This area we were hunting in is also known as a good place to find the deadly Cobra, both the regular and the King Cobra are found all over this region of the Himalayan mountain range. The first glimpse of a Cobra was on one of my hunting forays. I was tired from walking all day and was nearly back to the camp. I had just knocked a spider off my chest and had started walking around a curve in the trail. I saw something moving on the ground ahead on the trail and looked closer. The black stripe across the trail was moving at a slow pace and was getting smaller. I never did see all of it because the head part was already off the right side of the trail when I first saw it; the rest, about five feet of it, slowly disappeared into the brush on the right side of the trail. I asked Jim what it was and he held his hand up cupped like the neck of a Cobra. I thought it was too big for a Cobra, and he told me that there were two sizes of Cobras, one like the snake charmers use and one that is called a King Cobra. Which is a lot bigger than the other. I was glad that it had disappeared into the brush. While he was talking, he told me that there were bigger snakes, like the Pythons in this area also, but that we probably would not see one if we were careful, He said they like the rocky ledges and caves.

The next day, after breakfast, I took my gun and went out on the trail that led upward away from the camp. I did not want to hunt very far from camp without Jim, so I only went about half a mile up the mountain and then found a spot that I could just sit and wait and see what would come by. It was a large tree and the roots were up out of the ground around the base of the tree. It made a very good hiding place so I cleaned the brush out of it and made myself comfortable. Nothing could approach me from either side or back. It limited my area of vision but I felt a lot safer.

A few small birds flew by me a few times and once I saw a large Butterfly in the limbs of a large tree. It flew down out of the lower leaves and fluttered around for a while, then flew back up into the leaves. It was as big or bigger than our Butterflies here in the states and was, or looked to be, about the same color as our yellow and black Swallowtail Butterflies of the eastern U.S.

There was a large tree about fifty feet or so further up the mountainside that I could see clearly. As it happened there was very little underbrush around that particular tree and I could see the root system and the surrounding area very well. After a two and a half hour silent vigil, I caught sight of movement at the base of the tree; a few seconds later there appeared the head of a small cat. He was peeking over the top of one of the large roots that spread out from the tree base. If I had not known better, I would have thought I was back home looking at one of our gray and black striped cats. It was Identical in color, size and looks. It stayed there looking all around, not making any sound. When it's searching eyes found mine, it stayed real still, not moving, just looking at me. Then, suddenly, its head disappeared and it was gone. There was never a sound.

In the jungle where life can be gone in a flash, everything must be very careful and ever alert for anything new or different. If any animal that is hunted by another animal makes one mistake, it is usually fatal. There very life depends on their seeing the predator before it sees the prey. Anything new or different sends them into hiding or running away. They may look back out of curiosity when they have reached a safe distance, but they usually keep going till they are really out of there. I found out later that particular species of cat are found over a large area of the foothills.

If I had not been so well hidden, kept so quiet, and been so alert, I would not have seen the cat ease his head and eyes up over the top of the large root. I saw him before he saw me, so I could have shot him if I had so desired. If I had scratched my ear, swatted a mosquito, coughed, or made any kind of movement or sound. He would never have peeked over the root. He simply would never have been seen. When he had seen my eyes looking at him, he immediately knew I was alive and so, an enemy. I think if we had not made eye contact he would have watched me for a while before he ran, more out of curiosity, than fear. I'll never know.

The next day I received a radio request to investigate an old plane crash. It appears that an army cargo aircraft had exploded while flying over these foothills during the war. Some of the crew had found their way down out of the hills to civilization, but some of them were still missing in action. I was to work it in to some of my hunting trips if I could and report any of my findings.

The area of the crash was about fifteen miles southwest of our campsite, as the crow flies, so to speak. That would mean about thirty or more over these mountains by foot. After talking to the local natives, I found out that some of them had been there and knew the way to the wreckage of the aircraft, or what was left of it. Jim said that he knew the trail. As it turned out there was no trail, just a trail of cut marks through the jungle that had been made when someone had went to see what was left of the plane. Many of the villagers had heard and seen the plane explode and drop out of the sky. It had burned completely on impact, with the exception of the right wing, which had remained intact after it had broken off at the no. three engine. The explosion had been at night so it was visible from thirty thousand feet down as it fell.

Jim and I took off the next day. Both of us carried backpacks. Together we carried six days of food. No rifle, just my sidearm, a forty-five-caliber pistol. The food consisted of mostly rice with some canned meat to mix with curry and eat. Jim carried a blanket to use at night for sleeping and I carried a blanket and a jungle hammock with complete covering to keep the mosquitoes out. There were always trees to tie the hammock between.

There were two mountain ridges between our camp and the ridge with the plane on it, so we started directly toward the site, or where we thought the site was and took off down the mountainside. We went almost directly straight down the mountain and the going was fairly easy going down. When we reached the valley bottom we saw that the hill going up on the other side of the valley was rather steep. We decided that we would walk up the valley for a few hundred yards. By doing that we could climb the first ridge at an angle that would make climbing the side of the ridge a lot easier. Jim said that we could connect with the old trail of cut trees at the top of the ridge and follow it from there.

If you have to climb a steep hill or mountain, you'll want to make it easy on yourself. By climbing at an angle of twenty or thirty degrees relative to the level at the bottom, you make it a lot easier than trying to climb straight up the side of the mountain. I noticed that most of the trails used by the natives were cut into the mountainside that way. When they arrived at the top of the mountain they then kept to the top, as long as they could, toward their destination. On the top of the ridges there were no leeches or mosquitoes to worry about, and not many of those large yellow and black spiders. I liked that part.

Even traveling that way, we came across some very steep area where we had to pull ourselves up the hill by grasping small trees or rocks to keep from slipping or falling back or down the side of the mountain, it sometimes got very rough. We could not slide very far; there were too many trees in the way.

When we finally reached the top of the ridge. Jim looked around for a while then walked along the ridge looking for the cut trees that he knew were around close by. A few minutes later he located an area that had some cut trees in it. It was near the lunch break time, so we sat down and rested for about half an hour before starting on.

The trail down the other side of the ridge was angled a little better and the downhill walk was a lot easier. Whoever had made it and cut the little trees was thinking that he would have to climb back up the same way he was going down, so he made it easy as possible.

As we were walking down the side of the ridge we began to hear something making a disturbance in the trees below. They were ahead and below us on the side of the ridge. We were trying to be as quiet as possible and still go on our way. It was a tribe of Rhesus monkeys, eating and playing in the treetops. We were almost directly under them before they discovered we were there. One of them screamed and the whole tribe made a terrific racket as they took off through the treetops. It was quite a sight. They were soon out of sight and hearing.

We were making very good time so when we reached the bottom of the valley, we kept on following the cut tree trail on up the other ridge. We wanted to be far enough up the side of the ridge to be out of reach of leeches and mosquitoes for the nights sleep. As it happened, there was a very nice spring with good fresh water about half way up the side of the second ridge. The trail was long and was fairly easy to follow and as it began to get shadowed by the sun we knew we had better start looking for a place to camp. We reached the spring and decided it was the place. There was a fairly level area around the spring. Good enough for a campsite I found a couple of trees the right distance apart and put up my hammock. Jim started a fire and put on a pan of water to get hot for cooking the rice.

Tiger in the Area

I walked over to look over the spring. It was very deep and crystal clear. The gravel at the bottom was very clean and looked like it had been washed dozens of times. Above the spring there was a ledge that the spring water came out over and then dropped about ten feet to the pool of water we were beside. It was a beautiful waterfall. It made a lot of noise too as the water came down and splashed into the pool below. As I stood there looking at the beautiful pool and surroundings, I noticed a muddy section of the ground where the pool overflowed and went on down the side of the mountain. There in the soft mud were the pugmarks of a large cat, a very large cat. They were very clearly imprinted in the soft mud. I put my hand down over one of them and the print was bigger than my hand. Only one animal, a Bengal Tiger, could have made it, a very big one, and the prints were very fresh.

I called to Jim and motioned him over. I did not have to show the prints to him, he saw them as soon as he was close enough. He grinned and told me that I was not to worry. Tigers did not kill people very often and this one would not harm us. There was plenty of other game that the Tigers liked in the area. I sure hoped he was right. The evening meal consisted of boiled rice with a sauce of canned beef and curry seasoning over it. The natives use a lot of curry powder and cayenne peppers in their food. Sometimes they really make it very hot. The curry and beef was really good. He just made enough for the two of us, as he wanted to make sure all of it was disposed of and there would be no aroma in the area to bring the Tiger back or any other animal that might be in the area. The cookware and the utensils were cleaned in the spring so that all the smell of food was washed down the mountainside in the spring runoff. Needless to say, I did not sleep too good that night.

The next morning after a cup of instant coffee and some hard cookies we were off on our way up the side of the mountain to the top of the ridge. Due to the angle that the trail was going up the side of the mountain, we were making very good time. The sides of this ridge were not very steep so it was not hard to keep good solid footing. As we had left early, we reached the top of the ridge well before noon. We had been heading west on our way up. Now we were to head east as we went down the other side of this ridge. That would take us back in line for the crash site.

As alert as the animals of the jungle have to be to live, we saw very few as we walked the trail. They saw or heard us long before we could see them. It was not a quiet walk, for the noise of the jungle is fairly constant. Now and then we could hear the scream of a monkey or the loud call of a Hornbill I mentioned before. The big black bird with the yellow Ivory beak that was nearly as long as the bird itself. There were several of them in the area for we could see them flying over the high canopy of trees, every once in a while. They were always in pairs, as Jim had said, the Hornbills mate for life and live several years, unless a predator kills one of them.

We reached the valley floor early in the afternoon and stopped to rest a little. The water was cool and it was out of the sun. I sat down on a large rock, took off my backpack and looked around. I noticed some color in the leaves of some ferns and other green foliage that was on the side of the narrow valley. The area was moist and damp where the runoff of a spring further up the side of the mountain came down.

I got up and walked over to see what the color was. When I was closer I could see that it was an orchid, at least it looked like an orchid I had seen in the greenhouse back home. Only it was different color and a little smaller. It had the same shape and dainty leaves. I had the urge to pick it, but changed my mind and left it there. It would die if I picked it and I did not want it to die, maybe it would grow bigger and make more flowers. There is a lot of beauty in nature and I liked it that way.

A few minutes later we started the uphill climb to the top of the third ridge where the wreckage of the plane was supposed to be. The trail was at a nice angel to climb and was not very steep. We kept at a steady, but rather slow pace, which we could keep up for a longer time, and not become too tired As we were almost directly below the crash site, our path would be like a large letter V lying on it's side against the mountain. We would go east until we were halfway up the side of the mountain, then west back to the spot of the crash. That would make the climbing much easier and we still had plenty of time until dark. As it happened, that was pretty much the way the old cut tree marks went. We deviated a little, but followed pretty much the old trail.

Later that afternoon, as we were nearing the top of the ridge, we began to see pieces of metal and two bright yellow Oxygen bottles that had been inside of the doomed aircraft. The ground leveled off considerably and it appeared that the top of the ridge was a lot wider and flatter on top than the other ridges we had crossed. As anxious as I was to reach the scene of the crash, we came to a spot about one hundred feet below the top of the ridge and found a very good level spot for a campsite. We decided to set up camp and as it was getting late, decided to wait till morning to climb the last hundred feet to the crash site.

Tiger in Camp

Jim picked a good site for the fire and started one. I found a couple of trees that were the right distance apart for my hammock and tied it up good. After the fire was started, I noticed Jim was carrying a lot of small brush and tree limbs and putting them close to the fire; presumably to keep the fire going all night. He usually slept near the fire, on the ground. I guess both for warmth and safety.

"Hey Jim" I ask, "Why the brush pile"?

He replied, "Maybe Tiger come, he afraid fire, he come, I make big fire."

I had been wondering about that Tiger. Would he trail us? The only weapon I had was the side arm and it would be of little use against an animal that big, unless I was real close. I did not want to get that close to that Tiger. Even with a killing shot, he could kill me easily before he died from the gunshot wound.

After a meal of curried beef and rice we sat around the fire and talked. Jim did not seem overly concerned about the tiger. He said that the tiger was probably curious about us and he had probably been following us since we had camped at the spring. We tried to keep the smell of food to a minimum, but we still were sweaty and I am sure he could scent us from a distance downwind. When the wind was calm, he could scent us from almost any direction, as the air currents were moving in nearly every direction. Due to the heat of the sun and the depth of the valleys, the air currents move up the side of the mountain, then down the side, depending on temperature.

I finally told Jim that I was going to bed. I was a little concerned about the possibility of the Tiger showing up, but there was nothing to do about it. My jungle hammock was a large canvas hammock with a mosquito net sewn like a tent the full length and width of it, up to about three feet above it. I would be completely surrounded by netting with a zipper closing along one side and one end. I crawled in and closed the zipper and went to sleep.

I do not remember what time it was, but I was suddenly awakened by Jim shouting and hollering. I woke up and looked toward the fire. The flames were shooting up several feet high and Jim was throwing the pile of brush he piled beside the fire, onto the fire. As he did that he was yelling and shouting. I looked around to see what he was yelling at, and on the other side of the fire, in the light from the flames, there was the large head and part of the shoulders of a very large Tiger. It was not directly across the fire from me, but off to the left a little and I could plainly see the large Orange and black body of the tiger back as far as it's front legs. There were some white lines in the face. I tried to find my pistol. I had put it under my pillow, but it had slid down in the hammock and was somewhere under my blanket and me. The tiger could not see me, due to the mosquito net. He could not see through it. If I stayed still it would not notice me. He was watching Jim throw the wood on the fire. He would look at Jim, then at the fire. He did not look the least bit scared. After looking things over for about two or three minutes, he just backed up out of sight and disappeared. He had not looked in my direction at all, just Jim and the fire. It was by far the biggest cat I had ever seen. It had probably been following us since the spring and was just curious. At least that is what I hoped.

The tiger may have already been to my side of the fire. There is no way of knowing. My jungle hammock was pretty long and was strung between two trees. It was not very close to the fire. Of course I tied it as close as I could but the trees had to be a certain length apart in order to keep the lowest part from hitting the ground.

The Hammock was strung pretty tight but I still slid down to the center of it while I slept. The tiger could have come in from my side of the fire and smelled the hammock to see what was in it. Then backed off and went around to the other side to watch Jim as he dozed by the fire. I'll never know.

I do not remember Jim telling me what he was doing when he first saw the tiger. He must have told me, but all I can remember is that his yelling woke me up and when I looked out through the mosquito netting I saw him throwing the brush he had brought in onto the fire and it was blazing high into the air, all the time yelling at the top of his voice. I knew it was because of the tiger and I looked for it and there it was, to the left and on the other side of the fire.

After the tiger had left, we sat and talked for a while. To tell the truth I was a little hesitant to get out of the hammock and show myself. I did not know how far the tiger had gone, for all I knew, it might be out there, watching, all night. Jim kept the fire going pretty high for the rest of the night, and I did go back to the hammock and slept till morning. Jim stayed awake the rest of the night.

After a cup of instant coffee and some hard cookies the next morning, Jim and I climbed the short distance to the top of the ridge and found the remains of the doomed aircraft a hundred yards to the east of where we had camped, but on the top of the ridge. The ridge was about two hundred feet across and there was a little dip in the surface of the ridge. The burning aircraft had plunged straight down through the tops of the trees, nose first and had stayed in that position and burned completely. The right wing had broken off at the No.3 engine area. It had been a four engine cargo aircraft, loaded with supplies and equipment on it's way to China. The right wing was just far enough away from the fire that it did not melt the Aluminum structure of the wing. The No.4 engine nacelle was still there. The No.4 engine, as well as the No.3 engine, was missing. I never did locate the left wing or any sign of the No.1 & 2 engine.

Where the nose of the aircraft had hit the ground was a large pile of melted aluminum with brass cartridge cases sticking out of it. It had evidently been carrying a cargo of ammunition. There was no sign of the tail section or any other parts of the fuselage. On one side of the large pile of aluminum at the bottom of the pile I could see a couple of cylinders of one of the engines. There were no marks to tell which one. Beneath that engine I found a set of dog tags. They had been worn by one of the occupants of the aircraft. There were no signs of body parts, just the chain and tags. I do not remember the name on the tags, it was too long ago, but I took them back to camp and turned them over to military authorities, with my notes.

I searched the entire area without going too far down the backside of the ridge. There were several more Oxygen tanks, all painted yellow. There were also several Items of clothing and personal belongings scattered all around the area. Nothing important. In one area of trees, there was an open parachute caught in the high canopy of limbs. The chute was hanging empty and the belt was still fastened together, for some reason. It was out of reach from the ground and we could not get to it. It is probably still hanging there.

I made notes of everything and took nearly the whole day doing it. In my estimation, the explosion took place very high in the air and scattered parts over a large area. Both sides of the ridge had parts lying on the ground, and some parts could have been blown into the valley on the side we did not come up. It was an interesting experience, and one that I will remember always. I imagine that the first natives to arrive at the scene took some souvenirs, but that is something we will never know.

We called it a day and returned to camp for a meal and some rest. We had not much to tell, a lot of unanswered questions.

We took off early the next morning and arrived at the spring just before dark that evening. The return trip was uneventful. We heard a tribe of monkeys on the side of the second ridge, but they were too far away for us to see. At the end of the fifth day we returned to camp. We never saw the tiger again. I knew that Jim was concerned, but he never volunteered any information and I never ask. I wondered how he had known the Tiger was in camp. He never told me. He must have been awake watching.

I enjoyed those five days immensely. Seeing the wild Orchid was a plus. Every time I descended into the moist valley bottoms, my eyes were searching for orchids and I saw many more before I left the mountains. There was not much variety, but they were all beautiful. There was also a fruit tree that I saw occasionally which had beautiful red flowers growing next to the limbs, not on the branches. Jim told me that the fruit was good to eat, but I never saw any. I love the jungle, but I do not think that I will ever get to go back. It was not quiet, like our woods here where the climate makes the leaf changes. There the leaves are changing all the time and there is that continuous noise all the time in the background.

Jim said he knew where there was an apple tree that the deer liked to go to eat apples. The catch was that they only arrived at the tree just before dark, and it was several hours walk to where the tree was. I did not want to be caught away from camp after dark, as trying to find my way back to camp was very tricky. It seems that the air currents flow up out of the valley at night and down into the valley during the day. I talked to Jim about it and he said there was an area we could camp in a few hundred yards from the apple tree. The spot was beside the stream that flowed down the valley. Of course there were mosquitoes, but I had some strong repellent and a bottle of salt water for the leeches. We made camp and I left Jim there and walked up the streambed to the apple tree. Before I reached the spot where the tree was I left the streambed and climbed up the bank so as to be up wind of the tree area. I had to be able to see under the tree where the deer would have to be to eat the apples. I found a spot and sat down to await the deer.

It seems that the leaves do not make as much noise in the valley as they do up where they get a lot of sun. Perhaps it is the moisture content that keeps the noise down, because it became very quiet in the valley as evening came on. The apple tree was surrounded with dense grass on the ground. Under the tree, the grass was all trampled down from the deer looking for apples. It was not long before I heard something coming through the grass on the opposite side of the tree. Whatever it was, it would take two steps, stop, be quiet for a few seconds, then take three steps, stop for a few seconds, then take two steps, stop and listen, then take three steps, stop and listen, all the time listening and using it's sense of smell, trying to hear or smell anything that might be laying in wait for it. Like I was. I was not moving so it could not have caught me moving when it stopped so suddenly. The way it was approaching the tree kept sounding closer and I was watching the spot under the tree. The sound in the grass grew closer and closer until I knew it was about to come out into the open section. The noise stopped and I waited. Then the noise in the grass started again, the same pattern. It grew weaker and weaker until I could hear it no more. It must have scented a little of my breath or something, for it was too suspicious to venture into the open under the tree. Like I said before, animals that live in that environment only have to make one mistake, and they die.

The animal had probably been one of the little Barking Deer that live in that area. They are only about fourteen or fifteen inches in height, but when they bark they sound like they are big as a big dog. On the way back to the camp and Jim, I had to pass a high bank that was above my head. I had been walking on the sand of the streambed and making no noise, when all of a sudden I heard this loud bark right above my head on the bank of the stream. It startled the daylights out of me (so to speak). It was too dark to see and the bank was too high to see over. I stood still and watched to see if I could see anything. The little deer never showed itself and I went on to camp. Jim said he heard the little deer bark, but he did not see it either.

We slept there all night then returned to camp the next morning.

Back Home

When I was hunting here in the United States I thought I was a pretty good hunter, I usually got what I went after. A few days in the jungles of Asia set me back a lot. Those animals outsmarted me at every turn. I did not feel so bad after I had talked to some of the chiefs of the villages. They told me that each village was allowed one gun and they had one or two good hunters. When their hunter took the gun and went hunting, they sent a dog trainer and his dogs along to drive the Deer to the hunter.

After I left the hills and returned to the United States and became older, I began to realize just how foolish I had been to go into the jungle as I did. That Tiger could have killed me any time it wanted to. I was lucky. It just did not want to bother with me. I have read since, that most wild animals do not like the taste of humans. Lucky for us, I guess. That particular tiger had probably killed a native at one time and just did not want another. I am sure that if it had wanted to, it could have grabbed Jim when he was sitting by the fire and carried him off into the jungle. When I was there with the Air Force, during WWII, an eleven-foot (Nose to end of tail) tiger came into the camp at night and carried a mechanic by the head, out of his bed and into the jungle and ate part of him. The commander put out guards and when the tiger came back for another man. He was shot by one of the guards. The tiger had walked right into the tent where two soldiers were sleeping and picked one up by the head and dragged him out. The Jungle is a different world.

I have drifted from what this book is supposed to be about: Why do we hunt. There are many people in this world that have never been in an evergreen forest or a dense jungle, so they can not be expected to understand what we see in the act of going out into the hot, the cold, the mountains with the rocks and the many other perilous places that we go into in pursuit of some animal or whatever. Having said that I will say also that they should not then judge anything relative to the hunting procedures methods etc. that we hunters engage in.

We do it because we love the natural environment and we love being involved with nature. The pleasure that we derive out of walking through the fields, woods, hills, mountains and yes, even the jungle, we figure is worth every moment of our time.

Walking up the side of a mountain is hard work and in some instances is dangerous, very dangerous, but we think it is worth our time and effort. When we reach the top and stand on it looking out through the trees, if we were in the jungle, and we can see for miles to the valley below and trace the path of the stream or river that flows on its way to the sea. We can see one of the villages on the side of the mountain opposite us. Built on a plateau jutting out from the mountain, halfway up, to be above the mosquito and leech levels. We can watch the black Hornbills fly past below us, two of them, flying together.

Those people in New York City, that never get to see anything but the city or their condo in the Islands, can not imagine the feeling of walking through the jungle where you cannot see more that a few feet in front of you, with the underbrush nearly three feet high on both sides of the trail, where there is no way of knowing what may be laying along the trail waiting for something to come by within striking distance. Of course there is danger, but you could slip in a New York stairway or escalator and break a leg or arm. There is danger everywhere as well as pleasure. It is up to the individual to find what he or she likes and then pursue it.

The hunters who like to hunt the western states have a variety of options and a full scale of places and things to hunt. Any one of the western states will have a lot of beauty and a variety of game to hunt. All will have strict rules and regulations and a high range of license fees. The license fees reflect the cost of regulating and managing the national parks, wild game control and paying the salaries of the wildlife employees. There is a lot more to it than that, but you get the Idea. Without the help of the many thousands of hunters that purchase licenses each year, the wildlife service would be in real financial trouble and the people in New York City would complain about their taxes being raised. Hunting licenses are not cheap. They range from five or ten dollars to several hundred and in some cases, thousands of dollars every year. The money accomplishes two things. It keeps thousands of people working and making a living. And the hunters keep the population of the animals within the limits of the habitat available to them. This in turn assures a healthy herd.

No hunter that I know of ever gets tired of seeing the wild things at play or just going about the business of finding food. Some of them store food in the fall in places that they will remember and then they will get it when they need it in the winter. Most of you know that the squirrel families most all of them, will work long hours in the fall of the year. They gather the seeds and nuts and store them under ground or in hollow trees for future use. A lot of the underbrush is started that way. A squirrel will bury dozens of acorns in the fall, but will not need all of them or will not be able to find all of them. As a result, when spring comes the acorn will sprout and will become a great oak someday. The same is true about a lot of the other bushes, trees and flowers. Some seeds the wind will carry and drop, but the animals and insects do a lot.

One day in the fall I was hunting with my Bow and I picked a site where the deer came down to the water to drink. I was, of course dressed in my fall camouflage coveralls and face netting with hat. I was sitting about forty yards from a small pond that was fed by a small stream that carried cool clear water. While I was sitting there a pair of Wood ducks came flying in and landed on the pond. They are beautiful things; the Male especially is very beautiful. I have always enjoyed watching the wild ducks of all varieties as they fed and played in the streams and ponds around where I lived. It is another pleasure of my "hunting" trips. The ducks are another of natures way of keeping the variety of plants, insects and also diseases spread around the country.

When they feed in one place, they fly to another place. They carry seeds, germs, etc with them. When they land on the next pond or river, the seeds, germs etc. wash off of them or are in their droppings and so are started in another place. The worms that now infect a lot of our fresh water fish were spread exactly that way. That is why it is recommended that all fish be thoroughly cooked above one hundred seventy seven degrees before eating. Whole schools of "Skip-Jacks", a salt-water fish, are filled with worms too.

The Wood duck I was watching in the pond is a different sort of duck. They like to land in trees and nest in them as often as they can. If they can find a hole or cavity big enough to nest in they will. When the young are hatched and grow big enough to walk real good they have to crawl out of the nest and drop to the ground, sometimes many feet and then follow their parents to the pond. They never seem to be hurt by the fall.

I do not hunt waterfowl any more, I used to along the New Jersey shore in the wetlands. The Canadian geese, Snow geese and Mallard ducks were plentiful there. I tried them roasted, but the flavor was too much like fish. Also they all were covered with lice, which I did not like to work with. I skinned them before I cooked them also. Something will have to be done about the abundance of the Canadian Geese, and possibly the Snow Geese. I think the predators and the hunters are not keeping control of the flocks and soon they will become a source of problems with disease and not enough habitats for them all.

Back to the "Hunting": Many a hunter, when on a Hunt for Elk, Moose, Caribou, Bear, or whatever has stopped on one of the mountain, or high hill, tops and just stood or sat there and looked out over the vast landscape. The beauty that lay before him is unforgettable, and he will remember it always. Whether it is a vast open plain or a deep valley between two mountains, where the sun never quite makes it's way into the jungle. There is beauty, like the Orchids I saw in the jungles of Burma.

A person may travel to any of the Grand National forests or National Parks around the world, and will see lots of beauty. That is why they are preserved, for their beauty and for the people to see.

That is not quite like being on a hunting trip and walking quietly along the top of a ridge and suddenly coming to a sharp drop off and finding that there is a large herd of Elk just below you completely unaware of your presence.

Many times I have been sitting quietly and had the pleasure and the surprise of an animal or bird come within a few feet of me and stay for a few seconds or a minute or two then take off and go somewhere else They did not know what I was, but they knew I was a different shape, one that they were not familiar with, so they left.

One winter day in Western Pennsylvania, I was sitting in my favorite hole in the ground by the tree roots. There was about a foot of snow on the ground and it was cold. The snow was the light fluffy stuff. I was not seeing anything and was just beginning to doze off a little when I heard a loud snort behind me. I knew what it was so I just sat there and began to turn my head, very slowly around to the left. I was sure it was a doe and I did not try to raise my gun. As my head began to bring my peripheral vision into the area behind me I saw that it was a small herd of deer. All were does and they were lined up, one behind the other directly behind me. The lead doe stood and looked at me, pawing the ground and trying to get me to move or something. I was evidently to small an animal to be afraid of. In that hole, my head was the only thing above ground level and she was not afraid of anything that small. When I did not move, she just turned and started back the way they had come. The other does did the same.

I just read some statistics of the 2004/2005 whitetail deer season. There were four hundred fifty thousand hunting licenses sold. There were only two hundred seventeen thousand whitetail deer shot and tagged in at the check in stations. This means that there were two hundred thirty-three thousand hunters that did not get to shoot a deer. You can bet that they all enjoyed the time spent in the woods trying to get a shot at a good Buck. They will all try again next year. These figures were for the State of Ohio alone. I just heard from the Ohio Division of Wildlife that there were Twenty-nine Thousand, eight hundred seventy four road killed white tailed deer reported in the year two thousand four. That does not count the ones that limped away to die later somewhere in the woods.

A rare sight when you are hunting is to see an Albino animal of any kind. I have seen albino rabbits and on the Outdoor Show, they showed pictures of an Albino deer, it was running with a small herd of whitetail deer. Up until two years ago I had never even heard that there was such a thing as a white, albino groundhog or woodchuck.

Then one day two years ago in the spring of the year when the flowers were coming out and all the young rabbits etc were testing their legs outside of the den. I was coming back from a quiet walk in the wooded area across the road from my house and I saw a white spot on the edge of the road by the curve. As I drew nearer, the spot moved and the little brown spots that were with it were moving too. I took my binoculars and focused in on the spots. They turned out to be four young groundhogs or woodchucks, whatever you want to call them. One was pure white and the other three were regular brown color.

Needless to say, I was really surprised. In all my decades of hunting and roaming the woods and fields of this country, I had never even thought about an albino groundhog, let alone see one. There it was, only about five or six inches long and pretty as a new spring flower. I watched it for a while until a car came along and they all scooted for the den, which was a large hole in the bank along the side of the road. I told my hunting partner and we both saw it several times during the summer. We were hoping that it would not get in the way of a fast moving automobile before the mother kicked it out of the den and it would leave the road area. Then it would be out of danger of the cars. It left the den and moved away from the road and back along a little stream that ran parallel to the road. There it hibernated for the winter and we saw it the next spring. As it's den was in the neighbors pasture where he ran sheep and cattle, the neighbor ask us to keep the groundhog population down as much as we could. The neighbor shot it one day and took it to a taxidermist for preserving. No one had believed us when we told them we knew where there was an albino groundhog. Now we had proof. There is also a photo of an albino buck deer, in full velvet that the neighbor took. The antlers look a little funny because of the velvet that covers them when they are developing. The antlers are shed in the winter and the new ones grow very fast in the spring and they are quite beautiful after the velvet leaves them and they become very hard and shiny. Both the groundhog and the buck deer also have the pink eyes of the true albinos.

In seventy years of hunting and being in the woods in the State of Ohio, it is a wonder that I never came across an albino woodchuck before. It may be that the Genetics were just so pure that it never happened before. I really do not know that much about it, I do know that in all that time I never saw one, and I saw a lot of groundhogs in that period of time. The whitetail deer have many more albinos. There are several in captivity not far from here, so the white skin or albino gene must be more prevalent in the deer population.

During the last ten or fifteen years, the art of bow hunting has grown to high levels. First it was the longbow, then the compound bow, then and the crossbow. I never used the longbow for hunting, maybe a little practice. I did buy a good compound bow and practice till I became proficient in the use of it for hunting.

Now there are thousands of bow hunters around the world that use nothing but the compound bow and hunt everything there is to hunt, anywhere in the world. They have hunted nearly everything in Africa, Alaska, Canada and probably everywhere they were allowed. Some have been hurt, but many have accepted the Challenge and won and now have the trophy on the wall of their den to look at and remember the challenge and the chase.

The use of a Compound bow to make a kill on a huge Bison Moose or Bear, especially a bear of any size is a very dangerous undertaking and requires cool nerves strong muscles and extremely good accuracy with the bow. The hunter must be very close to the animal he is pursuing to make a killing shot. In the case of bear he probably has another hunter to back him up with a gun if need be. A wounded bear would not be a good situation. I imagine a bear can probably run a good distance with an arrow or bullet in his heart if he is very angry. Sixty yards is not very far for an angry bear.

As far as hunting goes, the Eastern Cottontail shown above and the ring-necked pheasant give the hunters in the Eastern half of the United States the most pleasure. Along with the pleasure is a lot of good eating. Both are seasonal meat for the table of a lot of people, in the fall of the year, and always a meal for the predators.

Both can really test the co-ordination of the hunter as most are shot while on the move, and it takes accuracy and quickness to hit a moving target. Most areas in the eastern half of the country are well populated with both the rabbit and pheasant, more in some areas than others. Neither is in danger of being endangered, as far as I know. The rabbit is an elusive creature when it is running. Very seldom does it run in a straight line, giving the hunter a clear and easy shot. It usually makes quick turns and dodges from side to side as it flees. It is found nearly everywhere as you can see in the picture. That picture was taken in my front yard. I like to have them around. I have never eaten them, although people have told me they taste really good when fried like chicken. The neighbor's cats get most of the young when they come out of the nest and follow their mother around. The older rabbits can usually keep from getting caught, as they are constantly alert for predators and really move fast when they need to.

Most of the hunters in my area of the country look forward to the Whitetail Deer hunting seasons each year. I know I do. I like the Bow hunting the most. It requires a little more skill, I think, because of the skill it takes to get you closer to the target for a killing shot. A shotgun or a muzzle-loading rifle is very effective in longer range shooting. It is not necessary to get to within forty or at most fifty yards for a clean and killing shot.

One year I shot a trophy Buck, quite by accident on his part. It was opening day of the gun season. It was cold, not real cold but I put on my bright Orange coveralls and my orange pull overhead covering. I walked up a large hill on my friends' eighty-acre property. The hill had been stripped for the coal beneath it many years before and the shape of the hill had been changed, as it usually is when it has been stripped. The side of the hill looked like a giant staircase, with huge steps every forty feet or so.

Right on the top of the hill there were some wild grape vines in the trees and it provided a perfect hiding place. A hunter concealed in the vines would be hard to see from anywhere below him on the side of the hill. The hillside was covered with trees and more grapevines clear to the top. All of the leaves were off the trees and visibility was good for over one hundred yards for about one hundred eighty degrees to the east of my position, when I had finally settled in to wait and see what would show up. The "step" about seventy yards away was a deeper step than the ones closer to me. I was afraid that any deer walking around that step would not be in my line of sight. I had found a spot on the ground between two fallen trees that had a natural rise where my back would be if I sat down, so that is where I made myself comfortable. My head was about all that would show above the logs on either side of me. The hillside curved around me from my left to my right and I had a clear view down the hillside.

I was very comfortable in my lined coveralls and was daydreaming about a big buck deer coming around the corner to my right. My eyes would close, then open and make a sweep along the steps from left to right, and then close again.

At about five minutes to twelve o'clock noon as my eyes were making the sweep, I saw two sets of antlers moving along the deep step I told you about.

They were about seventy yards away from me, moving from my left to my right. All I could see was about ten or twelve inches of each set of antlers. I could not see any part of the bodies of the deer. They were moving steady, one behind the other. I could not shoot antlers. I raised the gun and followed them with the sights, hoping that they would come to a low place where I could see some of the target area. I knew by the size of the Antlers that they were both trophy size bucks. My heart was pounding and I don't remember even breathing. Looking down the barrel I could see a dip in the edge of the step and it looked like I would get a chance to make a killing shot if it was a deep enough drop in the ground level. As I was thinking and hoping, the big buck walked out into the opening and I had a clear shot. I eased back on the trigger and the gun fired. The deer disappeared, both of them. I never did find out where the buck that was following the one that I shot at disappeared. I did not even see where the one that I shot at went. I knew that by all indications I should have made a direct hit and that the deer should be laying down there somewhere.

I waited for five or ten minutes, then eased up out of my nest and walked down to where I had last seen the big buck. As I walked over the last step, near the bottom of the hill, I saw the big buck lying on the ground. He had run about twenty feet before collapsing and he was a beautiful sight for me to see. I hate to kill anything, but I do love fried Venison steaks during the winter and I only had one or two left in the freezer. Besides I had never shot what could have been called a "Trophy" buck and that was a beautiful set of Antlers. I am not much on having the heads of deer hanging on the wall, but I did want a picture of them. My friend had to use his tractor to drag the buck to my truck to take to the check in station. The buck was so big, my friend and I could not lift it to put it in the truck, and we had to slide it up a board. We had field dressed it out in the woods and tagged it, so we were not lifting the full body weight of the deer before field dressing. I should have taken it to the check-in station and had it weighed before I had field dressed it. I was so excited I could not think about the fact that it might be a record deer or that it might meet the Boone and Crockett requirements. I just checked it in and took it home to brag about and take some pictures. I was about the happiest man in the state of Ohio about that time. That deer was the biggest deer I had ever seen. The neighbor guy wanted the head and antlers to mount on a plaque for his den wall.

As far as hunting goes, the Eastern Cottontail and the ring-necked pheasant give the hunters in the Eastern half of the United States the most pleasure. Along with the pleasure is a lot of good eating. Both are seasonal meat for the table of a lot of people, in the fall of the year, and always a meal for the predators.

Both can really test the co-ordination of the hunter as most are shot while on the move, and it takes accuracy and quickness to hit a moving target. Most areas in the eastern half of the country are well populated with both the rabbit and pheasant, more in some areas than others. Neither is in danger of being endangered, as far as I know. The rabbit is an elusive creature when it is running. Very seldom does it run in a straight line, giving the hunter a clear and easy shot. It usually makes quick turns and dodges from side to side as it flees. It is found nearly everywhere as you can see in the picture. That picture was taken in my front yard. I like to have them around. I have never eaten them, although people have told me they taste really good when fried like chicken. The neighbor's cats get most of the young when they come out of the nest to play.

This evening I went for a short ride around a few back roads and on to some main roads too, looking for road kills. In a fifteen-mile drive, I saw four dead raccoon, three Opossum, three dead whitetail deer, one skunk, one muskrat, one house cat, and two rabbits. All of them were killed within the last two weeks. If they were older than that the Turkey vultures would have had them eaten by now. The Turkey Vultures are the dead meat clean-up crew. They do a pretty good job, but sometimes there is too much and they cannot eat it all fast enough.

I cannot understand these people that think we hunters are mean for hunting and trapping the "poor things". When the population of any one of the animals gets over a certain amount the road kill numbers get higher and higher. It is a waste of good warm clothing that could be made from the beautiful fur of the animals like skunk, muskrat, raccoon, opossum and even the rabbit. The deerskin, either buck or doe can be made into the softest gloves, wallets, purses etc. Buckskin jackets are beautiful and very warm in winter.

In the spring of the year when the new grasses and flowers and the new tree shoots are coming out, the deer have plenty of food everywhere and they can eat whatever they want. The does are heavy with young and as they are borne they cannot leave the area for a while. With plenty of food available they do not have to travel looking for food so they are content to stay in the one area. If it is near water, which it usually is they are content to stay in the one area. This in turn keeps them off of the roads they might have to cross to get to other food. The number of road kills will drop accordingly.

Last week there was an incident involving three deer walking out onto the highway in front of an automobile with a mother and two young girls inside. The mother swerved to avoid hitting the deer and collided head-on with an oncoming car in the other lane. Needless to say, the mother and the two young girls were killed instantly. The other driver was taken to the hospital severely injured. Dozens of accidents like that are happening more and more. The deer population must be kept to a safer level.

Where there is a trapping season, the road kill numbers may be lower than where there is no trapping. There are hunters that would like to trap, but due to the anti-fur campaign by the animal rights people the price of furs has dropped below the profit margin and not many hunters set traps anymore. The road kill numbers are climbing as an over population of fur bearing animals are slaughtered on the nations highways, and the fur is wasted. Like I mentioned before. Literally thousands of animals are killed on the highways each year. In the past year, two thousand four, there were twenty-nine thousand eight hundred seventy-four recorded road kills in the state of Ohio. That averages out to about eighty deer per day killed on Ohio's roads. Many are just crippled and wander off to die later after suffering for a week or so. We have proof that there were at least two hundred forty-six thousand eight hundred seventy four deer killed in the two thousand four hunting year. What if they had not been killed? If half were females and they each had one and one half young babies this spring, There would now be three hundred seventy thousand three hundred eleven new deer. That would have brought the total number of deer in the state now to over six hundred seventeen thousand and that is not counting the ones that were not shot or killed on the road during the year. Thank goodness they were killed. If they had not, think what the accident rate would have been this year. How many human lives would have been lost? They must be controlled.

Many times throughout the past fifty years, I have walked out into the wooded area near wherever I lived and sat down to think things over. After a lovers quarrel or a spat with my wife, trouble with the children or whatever. There is something about the quiet, the beauty of the area, the rustling of the leaves or the many other pleasant things you encounter when you are there that soothes the mind, takes your mind off of the problems and lets you just see the beauty of nature in all it's glory. You cannot just walk and think of other things because what your eyes are seeing keeps you aware of your surroundings. The pureness, the stillness, the part that is unknown, the fact that anything could happen or move at any time, the wonder of it all tends to ease the problems and makes them seem so trivial that you relax and put them in the back of your mind and begin to enjoy the present and your surroundings

Epilog

I just wish that the people that think hunters are just animal killers could experience the feeling that comes with enjoying nature in all it's glory, any time of the year. Maybe then they could see that the hunters are really the controlling factor in the game management of this country. Maybe then they could see that you can only put so many rabbits in a pen before they begin to kill each other or starve without enough food, as the little deer did a few years ago in Florida until the game management took over and started to manage the herd.

Population control and food plots are the things of the future, both with animals and people. We have only one earth and it is fast becoming filled up. For all to survive something must be done. The latest news programs are reporting that some people are already thinking about the problem. There will be a lot of losses, but there will be an outcome. With today's world, full of greed and power grabbing, the outcome will be hard to predict. There will be an outcome, but who knows where or when.

Best wishes,
Solbert